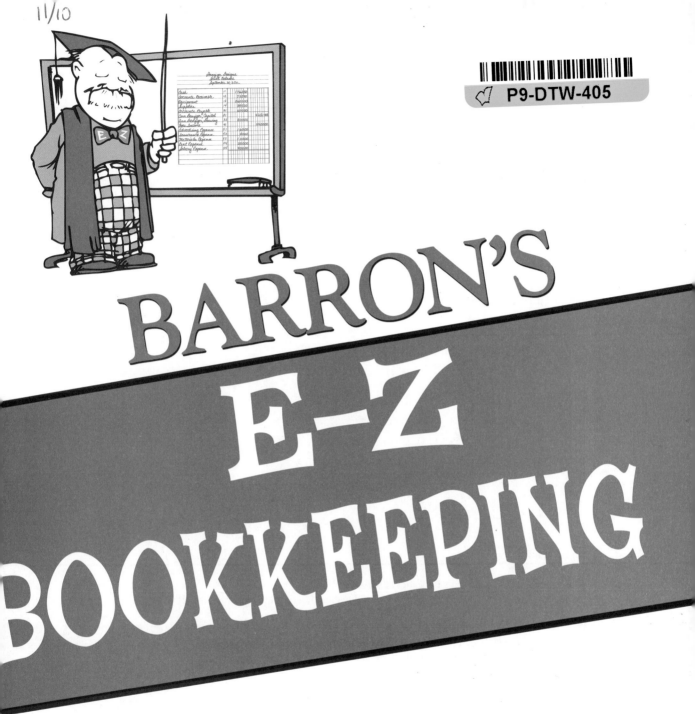

BARRON'S
E-Z
BOOKKEEPING

Kathleen Fitzpatrick, MBA
Associate Professor, Accounting
College of Business Administration
University of Toledo
Toledo, Ohio

Wallace W. Kravitz
Former Business Education Chairman
Mineola High School
Mineola, New York

BARRON'S

Better Grades or Your Money Back!

As a leader in educational publishing, Barron's has helped millions of students reach their academic goals. Our E-Z series of books is designed to help students master a variety of subjects. We are so confident that completing all the review material and exercises in this book will help you, that if your grades don't improve within 30 days, we will give you a full refund.

To qualify for a refund, simply return the book within 90 days of purchase and include your store receipt. Refunds will not include sales tax or postage. Offer available only to U.S. residents. Void where prohibited. Send books to **Barron's Educational Series, Inc., Attn: Customer Service** at the address on this page.

Note: The names of individuals and companies in this book are all fictitious and bear no resemblance to any real person or organization.

Fourth Edition

© Copyright 2010 by Barron's Educational Series, Inc.
Prior copyrights 1999, 1990, 1983 by Barron's Educational Series, Inc. under the title *Bookkeeping The Easy Way*.

All inquiries should be addressed to:
Barron's Educational Series, Inc.
250 Wireless Boulevard
Hauppauge, New York 11788
www.barronseduc.com

ISBN-13: 978-0-7641-4133-1
ISBN-10: 0-7641-4133-3
Library of Congress Control Number: 2009934835

Printed in the United States of America
9 8 7 6 5 4 3 2 1

CONTENTS

PREFACE

Knowledge of bookkeeping is a practical, useful skill set that will benefit everyone who works in a business. The many vocabulary terms introduced throughout the chapters familiarize students with "the language of business." Similar to acquiring foreign language ability, it is important to learn the terminology that is universally used in offices and publications.

This book presents the steps in the bookkeeping cycle in a logical, easy to follow format. Each chapter builds upon the knowledge gained in the previous chapters. Therefore, they should be completed in order. The sample companies are sole proprietorships: those with just one owner, but many of the concepts apply to any size business.

The clear explanations, examples, and practice problems have been classroom tested and are an effective method for learning. Since the best way to learn bookkeeping is to do it, students should complete each practice problem and check their work against the answers provided. If an error is found, review that section and complete the problem again. Continue until you have mastered each topic and can correctly complete the assignments. Repetition is the key to success!

I would like to thank all of my current and former students who have provided positive feedback over the past twenty years. They continue to inspire me as they tirelessly complete whatever assignments I place before them. They were always with me in spirit as I prepared this book and thought about the best way to present all of the necessary information. Each and every one of them contributed in some small way to my success.

Kathleen Fitzpatrick

Assets, Liabilities, and Owner's Equity

WORDS TO REMEMBER

- **Account** *each specific item* listed as either an asset, a liability, or a part of owner's equity
- **Accounts Payable** amounts owed to creditors
- **Accounts Receivable** amounts *due* from customers
- **Assets** all things of value that are *owned*
- **Business Transaction** a financial event that occurs, causing a change in two or more accounts
- **Investment** the owner gives his or her own money to the business, *directly increasing capital*
- **Liabilities** all debts that are *owed*
- **Owner's Equity** the value of one's *net worth, capital, or proprietorship*; the amount of assets remaining after all debts have been paid

SECTIONS IN THIS CHAPTER

- Definition of Assets
- Definition of Liabilities
- Definition of Owner's Equity
- The Fundamental Bookkeeping Equation

The fundamental elements of all bookkeeping systems deal with keeping records for changes that occur in ASSETS, LIABILITIES, and OWNER'S EQUITY.

Definition of Assets

ASSETS are all things of value owned by an individual or business. Personal assets may include cash on hand, as well as savings and checking accounts, an automobile, and a home. Business assets may include similar items, as well as amounts due from customers—ACCOUNTS RECEIVABLE—and a building owned, not rented.

EXAMPLES OF ASSETS–PERSONAL AND BUSINESS

A student's personal assets might include the following:

Cash on hand and in a savings or checking account
Clothing
Sporting equipment
Jewelry
Bicycle
Car

A family's personal assets might include the following:

Cash on hand and in checking accounts
Home owned, not rented
Furniture and furnishings
Investments in stocks, bonds, and/or land
Car

The assets of a small service-type business might include the following:

Cash on hand and in checking accounts
Building owned, not rented
Equipment
Supplies
Delivery truck
Land

Consider the following list of assets used by the Evergreen Landscaping Service, a company owned by Thomas Morales, the proprietor:

Cash	$1,450
Truck	21,000
Haulaway Trailer	1,500
Customers' Accounts	3,600
Equipment	43,320
Office Furniture	750
Supplies	645
Total Assets	$72,265

Customers' accounts refers to amounts owed to the business by its customers. They are assets because they will be turned into cash as payments are received. Customer Accounts are called ACCOUNTS RECEIVABLE, and will be referred to by that term in this text.

Definition of Liabilities

LIABILITIES are the debts owed by an individual or business. Personal liabilities may include unpaid charge account balances, as well as amounts owed on a home and/or automobile loan. Business liabilities may include similar items: amounts owed to creditors, and are called ACCOUNTS PAYABLE.

EXAMPLES OF LIABILITIES–PERSONAL AND BUSINESS

A student's personal liabilities might include the following:

Loan from parents to purchase a car
Balance owed on school yearbook or class ring

A family's personal liabilities might include the following:

Balance owed on home mortgage
Balance owed on installment purchases
Unpaid household bills—gas, electric, telephone

Consider the following list of liabilities owed by the Evergreen Landscaping Service:

Truck Loan, Island National Bank	$6,200
Unpaid Electric Bill	345
Mortgage on Building	41,000
Total Liabilities	$47,545

Definition of Owner's Equity

OWNER'S EQUITY is the net worth or capital of an individual or business. It refers to the amount of assets remaining after all liabilities are paid. To determine owner's equity, total all assets, then deduct all liabilities. The difference is the owner's equity.

EXAMPLES OF OWNER'S EQUITY

If a student's assets total $2,675, and liabilities total $450, the student's owner's equity equals $2,225:

Total Assets	$2,675
Less: Total Liabilities	– 450
Owner's Equity	$2,225

If a family's assets total $105,700, and liabilities total $44,960, the family's owner's equity equals $60,740:

Total Assets	$105,700
Less: Total Liabilities	– 44,960
Owner's Equity	$60,740

To determine Thomas Morales's owner's equity in the Evergreen Landscaping Service, follow the same calculation:

Total Assets	$72,265
Less: Total Liabilities	– 47,545
Owner's Equity	$24,720

Owner's equity can also be referred to as NET WORTH or CAPITAL.

The Fundamental Bookkeeping Equation

The relationship among the three elements of bookkeeping—assets, liabilities, and owner's equity—may be stated as follows:

$$\text{ASSETS} = \text{LIABILITIES} + \text{OWNER'S EQUITY}$$
$$\text{LEFT} = \text{RIGHT}$$

Assets are sometimes referred to as being on the LEFT side of the equation. Liabilities and owner's equity are on the RIGHT side.

Consider these in the following way:

ASSETS (everything of value *owned*)	LIABILITIES (all debts *owed*) plus OWNER'S EQUITY

An example of these three elements as they apply to Thomas Morales's truck is:

Truck

Original cost	$21,000	Balance owed to bank and	$6,200
		Morales's equity in truck	14,800
Total	$21,000	Total	$21,000

These three elements of bookkeeping may be stated as an equation:

$$\text{Assets} = \text{Liabilities} + \text{Owner's Equity}$$
$$\$21,000 = \$6,200 + \$14,800$$

or, simply,

$$A = L + OE$$

VARIATIONS OF THE FUNDAMENTAL EQUATION

When any two of the fundamental elements are known, the third can be found. If assets total $10,000 and liabilities total $4,000, owner's equity equals $6,000. Assets minus liabilities equals owner's equity, or

$$A - L = OE$$
$$\$10,000 - \$4,000 = \$6,000$$

If assets total $12,835 and owner's equity totals $7,000, liabilities equal $5,835. It is also true that assets minus owner's equity equals liabilities, or

$$A - OE = L$$
$$\$12,835 - \$7,000 = \$5,835$$

If liabilities total $16,000 and owner's equity totals $22,900, assets equal $38,900. It is also true that liabilities plus owner's equity equal assets. This reverses the sides of the fundamental bookkeeping equation:

$$L + OE = A$$
$$\$16,000 + \$22,900 = \$38,900$$

These examples illustrate the variations of the fundamental bookkeeping/accounting equation: $A = L + OE$. All of these are true statements, whether for an individual, a family, or a business.

YOU SHOULD REMEMBER

All assets are subject to *two* claims—

1. those to whom debts are owed

2. those of the owner(s)

In listing claims against assets, claims of those to whom debts are owed *always* come before claims of the owner(s).

BUSINESS TRANSACTIONS

A business transaction always results in at least two changes in the fundamental bookkeeping equation. This is called double-entry bookkeeping. Since both sides of this equation must be equal, a transaction that changes totals assets must also change either total liabilities or total owner's equity.

Each item listed as either an asset, a liability, or an owner's equity is referred to as an ACCOUNT and is given a title. Just like the title of a book, these accounts must be referred to by their exact title.

Do not add any extra words to the name of the account.

Examples of commonly used account titles and their meanings are shown below.

Assets

Cash—cash on hand and in checking or savings accounts
Accounts Receivable—amounts due from customers
Supplies—office supplies
Equipment—computers and other office machines
Land—specifically for land used in the operation of the business
Buildings—a building owned by the company

Liabilities

Accounts Payable—amounts owed to creditors, generally due in 30–60 days
Notes Payable—a bank loan
Mortgage Payable—a long-term loan for the purchase of a building

Owner's Equity

Capital—the owner's investment in the business

TRANSACTIONS INCREASING ACCOUNTS

Assume that Morales, the owner of the Evergreen Landscaping Service, borrows $2,500 cash from the Island National Bank. Money borrowed from a bank is called a note payable. The original bookkeeping equation showed:

Assets	=	Liabilities	+	Owner's Equity
$72,265	=	$47,545	+	$24,720

With the cash borrowed, the equation changes because the asset account, Cash, increases and the liability account, Notes Payable, increases:

Assets	=	Liabilities	+	Owner's Equity
$72,265		$47,545		$24,720
+ 2,500		+ 2,500		—
$74,765	=	$50,045	+	$24,720

This transaction resulted in two account increases: total assets increased and total liabilities increased.

Assume that Morales takes $5,000 of his personal cash to make an additional INVESTMENT in this business. When an owner contributes his personal asset to the business, this causes an increase in the capital account, which in turn, increases Owner's Equity. The equation now shows an increase in the Cash account and an increase in Thomas Morales's Capital account:

Assets	=	Liabilities	+	Owner's Equity
$74,765		$50,045		$24,720
+ 5,000		- - -		+ 5,000
$79,765	=	$50,045	+	$29,720

This transaction also resulted in two account increases; total assets increased and total owner's equity increased.

TRANSACTIONS DECREASING ACCOUNTS

Assume that Morales pays $1,000 cash to the Island National Bank as partial payment on the truck loan. The equation now shows a decrease in the Cash account and a decrease in the Notes Payable account:

Assets	=	Liabilities	+	Owner's Equity
$79,765		$50,045		$29,720
− 1,000		− 1,000		—
$78,765	=	$49,045	+	$29,720

This transaction resulted in two account decreases; total assets decreased and total liabilities decreased.

When an owner withdraws cash from the business for personal use, a decrease in cash and a decrease in owner's equity results, indicated by the drawings account.

TRANSACTIONS THAT INCREASE AND DECREASE ACCOUNTS

Some transactions may change two accounts on the *same side* of the equation. Assume that Morales bought $100 worth of supplies, paying cash for them. His Cash account decreased by $100, while his Supplies account increased by $100, with no change in total assets.

Assets	=	Liabilities	+	Owner's Equity
$78,765	=	$49,045	+	$29,720
− 100 + 100	=	—	+	—
$78,765	=	$49,045	+	$29,720

All transactions affect two (or more, as will be shown later) accounts. These changes may result in

(1) two increases

(2) two decreases

(3) one increase and one decrease

When transactions result in two account increases or two account decreases, totals on both sides of the fundamental equation change:

	A	=	L	+	OE	
(1)	$10,000		$2,000		$8,000	
	+ 1,500		+ 1,500		- - -	(two increases)
	$11,500	=	$3,500	+	$8,000	
(2)	− 500		− 500		- - -	(two decreases)
	$11,000	=	$3,000	+	$8,000	
(3)	+ 350					(one increase,
	$11,350					
	− 350					one decrease)
	$11,000	=	$3,000	+	$8,000	

YOU SHOULD REMEMBER

All transactions cause at least two changes in accounts. Either:

- two accounts increase, or
- two accounts decrease, or
- one account increases, and one account decreases.

KNOW YOUR VOCABULARY

Use each of the following words or terms in a statement relating to bookkeeping/accounting:

- Account
- Accounts payable
- Accounts receivable
- Asset(s)
- Business transaction
- Capital
- Debts
- Investment
- Liabilities
- Net worth
- Owner's equity

QUESTIONS

1-1 Classify each of the following accounts as an asset, liability, or owner's equity. Indicate on which side of the fundamental equation—left or right—each account would appear.

Account	Classification	Side
Example: Cash	Asset	Left
1. Delivery truck	1. (1)	2
2. Account payable, J. Glover	2. (3)	4
3. Paul Jacob, Capital	3. 6	5
4. Account receivable, K. Day	4. 7	8
5. Notes payable	5. 9	
6. Supplies	6. 10	
7. Equipment	7.	
8. Mortgage payable	8.	
9. Land	9.	
10. Buildings	10.	

1-2 Jack Calhoun's assets total $22,500; his liabilities total $7,500.
Mary Winslow's assets total $30,000; her owner's equity totals $25,000.
Which of these two individuals has a stronger "financial situation" or is better able
to pay all debts owed? What other information might be needed in order to give a
more definite answer?

1-3 Kenneth Lee operates a computer software business. He has a $16,000 cash
balance. New equipment needed to develop the latest type of programs for his
clients will cost $20,000. This will require some borrowing in order to pay for it.
Lee wants to use $6,000 of cash from his business, arranging a bank loan for
the balance.
   What will be the amount of the loan? What changes will occur in the fundamental bookkeeping equation as a result of the loan?

PROBLEMS

1-1 Complete each of the fundamental bookkeeping equations so that each will be a
true statement.

	Assets	= Liabilities	+ Owner's Equity
Example:	$ 10,500.00	$ 4,000.00	?($6,500.00)
1.	$ 15,750.00	$ 4,250.00	11,500.00
2.	24,900.00	3?.0000	$ 21,200.00
3.	62,500.00	5,000.00	12,500.00
4.	24,742.50	8,655.40	16,742.1
5.	31,070.92	8369.07	22,501.85
6.	175,882.35	68,951.39	?
7.	?	58,042.78	152,775.56
8.	229,953.11	?	189,638.63
9.	686,020.49	114,362.74	?
10.	?	330,172.41	786,570.87

1-2 Write the words *Increase* or *Decrease*, or both words, or *None*, to show any change(s) in TOTAL assets, liabilities, and owner's equity for each of the following transactions:

	A	=	L	+	OE
Example: Owner invests cash in business.	Increase				Increase
1. Paid balance due on loan.					
2. Paid cash for new calculator.					
3. Borrowed cash from bank.					
4. Received cash from customer.					
5. Sold old desk for cash.					
6. Transferred new desk from home to business.					
7. Bought new truck on credit.					
8. Withdrew cash for personal use					

1-3 For each of the following business transactions, add or subtract the amounts to update total assets, liabilities, and owner's equity:

Example: Karen Glaser, owner, invested $15,000 in a dry-cleaning business.

1. Bought $2,000 worth of equipment, paying cash.
2. Borrowed $7,500 from River National Bank.
3. Bought $450 worth of supplies, paying cash.
4. Bought a truck for $12,000, paying cash.
5. Made a $1,500 payment on loan from River National Bank.

		A	=	L	+	OE
	Start with	$14,250		$4,250		$10,000
Example:		+ 15,000		- - -		+ 15,000
		$29,250		$4,250		$25,000
	1.					
	2.					
	3.					
	4.					
	5.					

Owner's Equity Accounts

WORDS TO REMEMBER

- **Drawings** the account which records any *withdrawals* by the owner *for personal use*
- **Expenses** obligations incurred in connection with earning income or operating one's business
- **Net Income** amount by which revenue exceeds expenses, *when income earned is greater than expenses*; a *profit*
- **Net Loss** amount by which expenses exceed revenue, *when expenses are greater than income earned*; a loss
- **Revenue** money or money equivalent earned during the fiscal period

SECTIONS IN THIS CHAPTER

- Revenue Accounts
- Owner's Drawing Account

Revenue Accounts

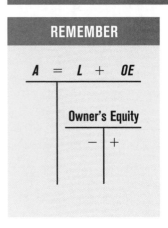
A business earns its income (or REVENUE) by selling merchandise and/or services. In this section, all revenue will be earned by charging fees for services performed by the business. The Evergreen Landscaping Service charges each customer a fee for the work performed on a regular basis—weekly or monthly. Special jobs, such as tree removals, are also a source of revenue. The term "revenue" will refer to various fees that are earned by services rendered to the customers of a business. In each case, they will be identified by a specific account title. Revenue is recorded following the *revenue recognition principle*, which states that revenues are recorded when they are earned. This is called the accrual method. It is not necessary for cash to be received in order for a business to record revenue.

EXPENSES

Obligations incurred in connection with the earning of revenue are called EXPENSES. These include such items such as advertising, rent, employees' salaries, and utilities (heat, light, telephone). Expenses are recorded when they are incurred or owed. Similar to revenue, it is not necessary for the expense to be paid before it is recorded. This treatment complies with the *matching principle,* which states that revenues and their related expenses should be recorded in the same fiscal period. This principle recognizes the fact that expenses are generally incurred by a business in order to assist in generating revenue.

NET INCOME/NET LOSS

If, during a fiscal period, the revenue earned is greater than the total expenses, the business will have a PROFIT or NET INCOME:

$$\boxed{\text{Revenue} > \text{Total Expenses} = \text{Net Income}}$$

If, however, expenses are greater than revenue, a NET LOSS will result:

$$\boxed{\text{Expenses} > \text{Revenue} = \text{Net Loss}}$$

(In these equations the symbol ">" means "is greater than.")

EFFECT OF REVENUE/EXPENSES ON OWNER'S EQUITY

In Chapter 1, you learned about the basic bookkeeping equation. At this point, the equation will be expanded by replacing owner's equity with its four components: revenues, expenses, drawings, and capital. In the expanded equation, note that revenues and capital are additions to owner's equity (indicated by the + sign). Expenses and drawings reduce owner's equity (indicated by the – sign).

Basic Bookkeeping Equation:

$$\text{Assets} = \text{Liabilities} + \text{Owner's Equity}$$

Expansion of Owner's Equity:

$$\text{Assets} = \text{Liabilities} + \text{Revenues} + \text{Capital} - \text{Expenses} - \text{Drawings}$$

At the end of a fiscal period, if revenues exceed expenses, the resulting net income belongs to the owner. Owner's equity will, therefore, be increased by that amount. If expenses exceed revenue, the resulting net loss also belongs to the owner. Owner's equity will, therefore, be decreased by that amount. In addition, capital refers to the value of the owner's investment in the business. Any additional investments will increase owner's equity. Drawings is an account used to record an owner's withdrawal of assets (usually cash), from the business for personal use, so it decreases owner's equity.

The expanded equation can be rearranged mathematically so that the two negative accounts (expenses and drawings), are moved from the right side of the equation to the left side. By adding expenses and drawings to both sides of the equation, it will be rebalanced.

$$\text{Assets} = \text{Liabilities} + \text{Revenues} + \text{Capital} - \text{Expenses} - \text{Drawings}$$
Add: Expenses + Drawings = Expenses + Drawings

On the right side of the equation above, Expenses and Drawings are cancelled out. We are left with the following:

$$\text{Assets} + \text{Expenses} + \text{Drawings} = \text{Liabilities} + \text{Revenues} + \text{Capital}$$

This is known as the expanded equation. It provides a logical and essential guideline for understanding future chapters in this book. Take the time to carefully memorize the expanded equation. Note that there are exactly three elements on each side of the equal sign. Let's examine how business transactions can affect revenues, expenses, capital and drawings.

Assume that the Evergreen Landscaping Service received $2,500 in fees last month, and expenses totaled $1,500 for the same period. All transactions were on a cash basis.

Revenues	$2,500
Less: Expenses	– 1,500
Net Income	$1,000

The accounts will change as shown below for the revenue received (*a*), and for the expenses paid (*b*). By the end of the fiscal period, the bookkeeping/accounting equation will have changed:

	Assets	+ Expenses	+ Drawings	= Liabilities	+ Revenues	+ Capital
a)	+ 2,500			=		+ 2,500
b)	− 1,500	+ 1,500		=	0	
Balance	1,000	+ 1,500		=	0	+ 2,500

Owner's Drawing Account

At any time, the owner of a business may withdraw cash for personal use, very much like a salary. WITHDRAWALS by the owner, however, are not included with other expenses. Instead, a separate account is opened for the owner's DRAWING ACCOUNT.

EFFECT OF WITHDRAWAL ON OWNER'S EQUITY

Any *withdrawal* by the owner *decreases owner's equity*. Note the transaction to record Morales's withdrawal of $500 cash.

This transaction changes the fundamental bookkeeping equation: $500 less cash (assets) and $500 less owner's equity, indicated by an increase in the drawings account.

Assets + Expenses + Drawings = Liabilities + Revenues + Capital

−500   +500   = 0

YOU SHOULD REMEMBER

- Income increases owner's equity.
- Expenses *decrease owner's equity*.
- Assets + Expenses + Drawings = Liabilities + Revenues + Capital

KNOW YOUR VOCABULARY

Use each of the following words or terms in a statement relating to bookkeeping/accounting:

- Drawings
- Capital
- Expenses
- Net income
- Net loss
- Profit
- Revenue

QUESTIONS

2-1 What are the sources of revenue received by each of the following service businesses?
a) A tailor
b) A beauty salon
c) An architect
d) A lawyer
e) A dentist
f) An accountant

2-2 What are some typical expenses paid by each of the businesses listed in Question 1?

PROBLEMS

2-1

(1) Using the expanded equation, enter the beginning balances for Puccio's Taxi Service, owned by Frank Puccio:

Assets:	Cash	$562
	Taxis (2)	28,000
Liabilities:	Notes Payable: Landia National Bank	6,400
	Accounts Payable: Wilson Garage	75
OE:	Frank Puccio, Capital	?

Additional accounts used by Puccio's Taxi Service:
Frank Puccio, Drawing
Fare Income
Gas Expense
Repairs Expense
Salary Expense

(2) Record the following transactions below the expanded equation.
a) Collected $250 in fares.
b) Paid Landia National Bank as partial payment on the note, $100.
c) Paid driver's salary, $200.
d) Withdrew cash for personal use, $300.

e) Collected $325 in fares.
f) Paid for gasoline, $45.
g) Paid Wilson Garage, $75.
h) Paid for taxi repairs, $40.

(3) Total the columns and prove the total of the left side equals the total of the right side.

Assets + Expenses + Drawings = Liabilities + Revenue + Capital

	Assets	+ Expenses	+ Drawings	= Liabilities	+ Revenue	+ Capital
Beg. Bal.						
a)						
b)						
c)						
d)						
e)						
f)						
g)						
h)						
Totals						

2-2

Rowena Tucker operates a messenger service. Her accounts show the following information:

Cash

462	75
300	75
200	300
600	95
200	140
250	100
	300
	25

Accounts Receivable

875	200
	250

Delivery Equipment

12000	

Supplies

60	
100	

Accounts Payable

25	1100

Rowena Tucker, Capital

	12297

Rowena Tucker, Drawing

300	
300	

Delivery Income

	300
	600
	200

Advertising Expense

95	

Telephone Expense

140	

Trucking Expense

75	
75	

2-2 Prepare a list that shows the balance of each account. (Add the left and right sides of each account. Subtract the smaller amount from the larger. The difference is the account balance.)

THINK IT OVER

James Lightfoot owns three sporting goods stores, each located in a suburban center near a large midwestern city. For several years he has had a net income. Last year, however, he had a small net loss. He is anxious to find the reason for this loss. Lightfoot maintains one set of records for his business. What would you recommend that he do differently, and why?

Recording Transactions in a General Journal

3

WORDS TO REMEMBER

- **Balance** the *value of an account* at any given time, as at the end of a fiscal period
- **Compound Entry** a *journal* entry that consists of three or more accounts, wherein the total of all debits equals the total of all credits.
- **Credit (cr.)** entries *on the right side* of any account
- **Debit (dr.)** entries *on the left side* of any account
- **Double-Entry Bookkeeping** a method of bookkeeping in which, for every transaction, *the amounts debited must equal the amounts credited* (Debits = Credits)
- **Journal** *a book of original entry* recording transactions in *chronological order*
- **Ledger** *all accounts*, taken together *as a group*, for the same individual or business
- **Simple Entry** an entry that consists of *one debit* that equals *one credit*
- **T-Account** an accountant's device, in the form of *a large "T,"* used *to analyze* debit and credit *entries* for each transaction
- **Voucher** a *source document* that is the *evidence of a transaction*

SECTIONS IN THIS CHAPTER

- Debits and Credits
- Journalizing Transactions

Debits and Credits

Although transactions can be recorded using the bookkeeping equation, as demonstrated earlier, it is not practical to use this method for several reasons. Businesses deal with many transactions every day. Consider the difficulty of tracking hundreds or even thousands of daily transactions by adding or subtracting from the equation's columns. The equation method also makes it difficult to track each of the individual accounts such as rent expense, salaries expense, etc. Because of these issues, bookkeepers use an alternative method for recording transactions. The expanded equation remains as a point of reference.

$$\text{Assets} + \text{Expenses} + \text{Drawings} = \text{Liabilities} + \text{Revenues} + \text{Capital}$$

Left	=	Right
Debit	=	Credit

Note that the left side of the equation must equal the right side after each transaction has been recorded. The terms *left* and *right* can be replaced with *debit* and *credit*. These are sometimes abbreviated as *dr* and *cr*. In bookkeeping, *debit* refers to the left side of the equation and *credit* refers to the right side. Be careful not to attach any other meaning to these terms.

Accounts that fall under the categories on the left side of the equation are referred to as debit accounts and those that fall under the right side are referred to as credit accounts. Therefore, all assets, expenses, and drawings are debits, and all liabilities, revenues, and capital are credits. For example, cash is an asset, so it is a debit. Accounts payable is a liability, so it is a credit. All of the accounts in a business can be referenced in this way.

Financial transactions can affect an account in two ways: increase or decrease. If revenue is received, cash will increase. However, if supplies are purchased and paid for, cash will decrease. The terms *debit* and *credit* refer to the side of an account that increases. Since cash is an asset and all assets are debits, this means that an increase in cash is a debit to cash. A decrease in cash is a credit to the cash account.

T-ACCOUNTS

Accountants often use a form called a T-account, because it resembles a large letter T, to illustrate the impact of a transaction on each account. The account title is written on top of the T. The left side is labeled *debit* and the right side is labeled *credit*.

Examine the Evergreen Landscaping Service's cash account, starting with an opening BALANCE of $1,450. This account has a title: Cash. The left side of an account is the DEBIT side; the right side of an account is the CREDIT side.

	Cash
Debit	Credit
+	–
1450	

All *assets* would appear in the same way—as *debit balances*. Since the cash account is on the left side of the expanded equation, cash will increase on the debit (left) side of its account, as indicated by the plus sign. A minus sign indicates that decreases to cash are entered on the right side.

Examine the T-account for Evergreen Landscaping Service's liability owed to Island National Bank. This account has a title: Note Payable. The left side is the debit side; the right side is the credit side. However, since Note Payable is on the right side of the expanded equation, it increases on the credit (right) side of its account.

	Note Payable
Debit	Credit
–	+
	6200

All *liabilities* would appear in the same way—as a *credit balance.*

Examine Morales's owner's equity account: Thomas Morales, Capital. The account has a title: Thomas Morales, Capital.

	Thomas Morales, Capital
Debit	Credit
–	+
	14720

The left side is the debit side; the right side is the credit side. Liabilities and capital are located on the right side of the bookkeeping equation, so increases to these accounts would be recorded on the credit side of the T-account, as indicated by the plus sign. Decreases to these accounts are recorded on the debit (left) side.

Journalizing Transactions

Rather than recording transactions using the equation method, accountants use journals to keep track of all financial transactions. A journal is a book of the ORIGINAL ENTRY, where complete information about a transaction is first recorded. Each page is numbered; columns provide space for a complete date—year, month, day; names of accounts debited and credited; posting references (to be discussed in Chapter 4); and amount columns for debits and for credits. Recall that every transaction must have at least one debit and one credit, so that the equation remains in balance and debits are equal to credits. When recording a transaction in a general journal, always put the debit account first and the credit account below it. All entries are recorded in CHRONOLOGICAL order as they occur. All information—the date of the transaction, the accounts involved, the amount of each debit and each credit—and any needed explanation are included in this book called the general journal.

JOURNAL   *Page 12*

Date		Account Title	PR	Debit	Credit
20__					
Sept.	4	Cash		1500 00	
		George Corbo, Capital			1500 00
		Investment			
	7	Supplies		100 00	
		Cash			100 00
		Check No. 418			
	10	Cash		2000 00	
		Notes Payable–Landia National Bank			2000 00
		30-day Loan, Note No. 25			

This general journal illustrates several transactions entered in chronological order on page 12, as noted in the upper right corner of the journal. The first transaction, dated September 4, is for a $1,500 cash investment in the business made by the owner, George Corbo. Before recording a transaction, think about which accounts are affected. Remember that all transactions affect at least two accounts. Consider whether each account is increasing or decreasing. Refer to the accounting equation to determine if the account should be debited or credited. When recording in a journal, each entry must have at least one debit and one credit.

At this point, you are ready to begin entering your information into the general journal. When the owner invests additional money in the business, both the cash and capital accounts are increased. However, cash increases with a debit (because it is on the left side of the equation), and capital increases with a credit (because it is on the right side of the equation).

Begin by entering the date the transaction occurred. The name of the month, with the year, is entered once and is not repeated until the next page of the journal. Only the number of the specific day is used unless the month changes. Under account title, enter the names of the accounts being affected. The debited account must be recorded first, and the credited account is written on the line below the debit. It is important to note the correct placement of each account title. Debited accounts are written right next to the line that separates the date column and the account title column, but the credited accounts are indented ½ inch.

This procedure makes it easy to scan a journal page and quickly identify which accounts are debits and which are credits. Dollar amounts are placed on the same line as the account title and in the corresponding column for debits or credits. After you have recorded an entry, check to be sure that the total dollar amount of the debits equals the total dollar amount of the credits. The next line of the journal can be used for a brief explanation of the transaction.

The transaction dated September 7 is for a $100 cash purchase of supplies. The supplies account increases with a debit and cash decreases with a credit to that account. The third, dated September 10, is for $2,000 cash borrowed from Landia National Bank. Cash increases with a debit and notes payable increases with a credit. Notes payable is used instead of accounts payable in situations where a formal legal document (called a note) has been signed. A note will include payment terms such as due dates and interest charges. Bank loans are usually in the form of a note.

SOURCE DOCUMENTS

As transactions occur, SOURCE DOCUMENTS are prepared as evidence of these transactions. The bookkeeper uses these *source documents* to obtain the information needed to create journal entries. They serve as a record of transactions that have occurred. In some cases, the source document may be referred to in the journal entry explanation. A source document is any prepared form or VOUCHER, such as a check or check stub, a numbered bill for services, or a memorandum of a transaction.

JOURNALIZING

Journalizing *begins with the source document.* The information on it tells the bookkeeping clerk all that is needed for the entry—the transaction date, the customer or vendor name, the dollar amount, and, if needed, a brief explanation. Here, for example, is a check stub for the payment of October rent in the amount of $500.

NO _173_ Oct. 1 20__			
TO _Ace Realty_			
FOR _Oct. Rent_			
AMOUNT _500.00_			
BAL.	6	253	15
THIS CK.		500	00
BAL.	5	753	15

The entry to record this transaction in a general journal is:

JOURNAL Page 8

Date			Account Title	PR	Debit	Credit
20__						
Oct.	1		Rent Expense		500 00	
			Cash			500 00
			Check No. 173			

This journal entry increases rent expense and decreases cash. Learn the rules of how accounts increase and decrease in order to properly debit and credit accounts. Knowing these rules simplifies the entire journalizing procedure. See the sample journal on page 27 for additional examples of journal entries.

The bookkeeping clerk records additional entries on the next page of the journal, starting again with a complete date:

JOURNAL   *Page 13*

Date		Account Title	PR	Debit	Credit
20__					
Sept.	15	Cash		50 00	
		Accounts Receivable (John Smith)		100 00	
		Fees Income			150 00
		Sales Slip No. 284			
	20	Equipment		800 00	
		Accounts Payable			
		Regional Supply Company			800 00
		Voucher No. 31			

On September 15, services were performed for a customer, John Smith, who was charged $150. He paid $50 in cash and charged the balance, $100. This transaction illustrates a COMPOUND ENTRY, where more than two accounts are debited and one account is credited. Notice, however, that the total of debit amounts equals the credit amount (50 + 100 = 150). The other entry illustrated is a SIMPLE entry—having only one debit equal to one credit. (800 = 800)

The entry on September 20 is for $800 worth of equipment purchased on account (on credit) from the Regional Supply Company. This is called a CHARGE purchase, as opposed to a cash purchase. The bookkeeper continues recording all transactions into the general journal as they occur during the month.

Notice that the debit account is always listed first in each journal entry. The account to be credited is indented. The amounts of the debit and credit line up with the account titles. Any explanation is listed below the last account title. The name of the month, with the year, is entered once and is not repeated until the next page. Only the day number is used unless the month changes.

Re-examine in T-accounts the transactions first explained on pages 8 and 9:

1. Morales borrowed $2,500 cash from the Island National Bank.

2. He invested an additional $5,000 cash in his business.

3. He paid $1,000 cash to the Island National Bank.

4. He bought for cash $100 worth of supplies.

A *partial* ledger for the accounts involved and the debits and credits for (1), (2), (3), and (4) above is shown as follows:

	Cash				Supplies		
	Debit		Credit		Debit		Credit
	+		–		+		–
Bal.	1,450	(3)	1,000	Bal.	645		
(1)	2,500	(4)	100	(4)	100		
(2)	5,000						

	Note Payable				Thomas Morales, Capital		
	Debit		Credit		Debit		Credit
	–		+		–		+
(3)	1,000	Bal.	6,200			Bal.	24,720
		(1)	2,500			(2)	5,000

Notice that each numbered transaction identifies a debit and a credit of equal amount. This is helpful in order to follow the system of double-entry bookkeeping. For every transaction, debits must equal credits.

YOU SHOULD REMEMBER

- In every transaction *debits equal credits*.
- Journal entries are listed *chronologically*.
- Debit accounts and amounts are always *listed first* in journal entries.
- Credit accounts are *indented 1/2 inch following debits*.
- Be sure that each journal entry has at least one debit and one credit.
- Verify that total debits = total credits.
- In every entry *debits equal credits*.

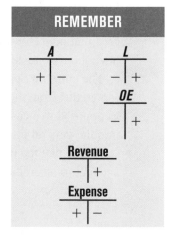

KNOW YOUR VOCABULARY

Use each of the following words or terms in a statement relating to bookkeeping/accounting:

- Balance
- Book of original entry
- Chronological order
- Compound entry
- Credit (cr.)
- Debit (dr.)
- Double-entry bookkeeping
- Journal
- Ledger
- Rules of debits and credits
- Simple entry
- T-account
- Voucher

QUESTIONS

1. If there are 250 transactions in one month, at least how many entries will there probably be in a *ledger* that month?

2. Why would a numbering or lettering system not be practical in recording entries directly in a ledger?

3. How does the journal entry identify the debit(s) part of any entry compared to the credit(s) part?

4. Are the following statements true or false?
   a) For *every* transaction, the account(s) debited equal(s) the account(s) credited.
   b) For *every* transaction, the account(s) increased equal(s) the account(s) decreased.

5. Explain your answer to 4(b).

6. What would be the normal balance of any asset account?

PROBLEMS

3-1 Using a general journal, page 7, record each of these transactions for Rose Klein, owner of a dress designing business:

October 2 Paid employee's salary, $175

      7 Received $600 cash for a design (design income)

    14 Paid $200 cash for supplies and material

    16 Borrowed $1,000 cash from the Veron Trust Co.

    21 Received $500 cash for a design

    23 Bought a new $360 drawing table (equipment) from the Textile Equipment Company. Paid $160 cash and charged the balance, $200.

    30 Withdrew $400 cash for personal use

    31 Received $100 cash from Mary Wu, a customer, in partial payment of her account. (She previously purchased a design on credit for $350).

3-1 *GENERAL JOURNAL* Page 7

Date	Account Title	PR	Debit	Credit

3-2 What would be a typical source document for each of the transactions listed in Problem 3-1?

3-3 Emilee Suzanne listed the following account balances:

Cash	$1,245
Equipment	3,670
Supplies	430
Accounts Payable:	
L.D. Brown	400
J.C. Tucker	175

(1) Open a ledger of T-accounts for each of these accounts, including one for each creditor.

(2) Open a T-account to record Emilee Suzanne's capital.
Remember: $A - L = OE$

3-4 Paul Jacobs listed the following account balances:

Cash	$1,305
Accounts Receivable	
D.R. Able	150
M.O. Jackson	225
V.L. Witten	85
Truck	15,750
Supplies	395
Accounts Payable:	
City Trust Company	1,250
H. & H. Manufacturing Co.	800

(1) Open a ledger of T-accounts for each account, including Jacobs' Capital.

(2) Prove that Assets = Liabilities + Owner's Equity

3-5 Kimberley Travis completed the following transactions last week:

Example: Paid Regal Bank, $150.

(1) Bought $75 worth of supplies for cash.

(2) Borrowed $1,000 from Regal Bank.

(3) Invested $2,500 cash in her business.

(4) Bought $500 worth of equipment from Bixby Company, agreeing to pay in 30 days.

Record the debits and credits for each of the above transactions in the following partial ledger. Beginning account balances are indicated. Identify each debit and each credit by the number of the transaction.

Cash		Equipment	
4075	*Ex.* 150	12500	

Supplies		Note Payable	
200		*Ex.* 150	2000

Accounts Payable		Kimberley Travis, Capital	
			14775

3-6 Using the transactions in Problem 3-5, indicate any increases or decreases in *total* assets, liabilities, and owner's equity.

Trans. No.	Assets	Liabilities	Owner's Equity
Example	Decrease	Decrease	
(1)			
(2)			
(3)			
(4)			

3-7

(1) Open T-accounts for Lori Luing, the owner of Luing's Answering Service, for the following balances, including her owner's equity:

Cash	$437.50
Accounts Receivable:	
H.L. Rhodes, MD	50.00
Mary Turner, MD	50.00
T.W. Vine, DDS	35.00
Equipment	2,650.00
Supplies	25.00
Accounts Payable:	
State Telephone Co.	215.00
Ace Electricians	65.00
Lori Luing, Capital	?

(2)   Complete each of the following transactions, indicating by letter the debits and credits:

    a)   Received $50, the amount due, from H.L. Rhodes, M.D.

    b)   Paid $65, the amount owed, to Ace Electricians.

    c)   Bought $75 worth of supplies, paying cash.

    d)   Invested $500 cash in the business.

    e)   Received $25 on account from Mary Turner, M.D.

(3)   Prove that Assets = Liabilities + Owner's Equity.

THINK IT OVER

Select any service-type business and consider the many different kinds of transactions that are carried on in any typical day. Think about the reason(s) why the owner is in business. What is his/her goal? What is the "profit motive" that keeps the owner going?

The General Ledger and Trial Balance

4

WORDS TO REMEMBER

- **Cross Referencing** a bookkeeping procedure in which the *journal entry posting reference* column *indicates the account number* that has been posted, and the *account posting reference* column *indicates the journal page number* of the original entry
- **Footings** tiny *pencil totals* of any column of dollar amounts
- **In Balance** refers to a trial balance with *equal column totals*
- **Out of Balance** refers to a trial balance with *unequal column totals*
- **Posting** the procedure of *transferring entries from the journal to the ledger*
- **Trial Balance** a two-column listing of all *ledger accounts* and their *balance*; if *debits equal credits,* the trial balance is *in balance*

SECTIONS IN THIS CHAPTER
• Posting Procedure
• Trial Balance

The system of recording transactions in a general journal does not replace the use of ledger accounts. At some point, each *amount* debited or credited in the journal must be transferred to the ledger accounts named in the journal entry. This step is called POSTING. Posting should be done on a regular—daily, weekly, or monthly—basis, depending on the frequency of transactions.

Posting Procedure

Every ledger account has a number assigned to it as well as a title. Each account appears on a separate page of the general ledger with a number that identifies the type of account. The numbering system follows a specific format in which asset accounts begin with 1, liabilities begin with 2, owner's equity accounts begin with 3, revenue accounts begin with 4, and expense accounts begin with 5. For a small business with a limited number of accounts, one possible numbering system is shown below.

Classification	Account Number
Assets	11–19
Liabilities	21–29
Owner's Equity	31–39
Revenue	41–49
Expenses	51–59

Larger businesses with more accounts would use a numbering system with 3, 4, or more digits. For example, cash might be account number 110.

JOURNAL TO LEDGER

The steps in posting a journal entry are as follows:

(A) Enter, for the account debited, the *amount* on the debit side of that account in the ledger.

(B) Enter the date—year, month, and day (thereafter, do not repeat the year and month).

(C) Enter the *journal page* number in the Posting Reference (PR) column of the account. The General Journal is represented by the letter G.

(D) Enter the *account number* in the Posting Reference (PR) column of the journal.

Repeat the posting procedure for the next account listed in the journal. Continue with each journal entry, posting debits and credits to each of the accounts listed. If the work of posting is interrupted, the bookkeeping clerk will always know exactly where to resume work—after the last posting reference *account number* in the journal PR column.

Just as debits must equal credits in each journal entry, debits must equal credits when posted to ledger accounts. The following journal entry will be posted to the accounts involved. (Assume that cash has an $800 debit balance (✔) from the preceding month.)

(C)
GENERAL JOURNAL   *Page 8*

	Date		Account Title		PR	Debit	Credit
(B)	20__ Oct.	4	Rent Expense	(D)	53	(A) 500 00	
			Cash	(D)	11		(A) 500 00
			Check No. 173				

GENERAL LEDGER

Account No. 11
Cash

	Date		Explanation	PR	Debit	Credit	Balance
	20__ Oct.	1	Balance	✓			800
(B)		4		G8		(A) 500	300
				(C)			

Account No. 53
Rent Expense

	Date		Explanation	PR	Debit	Credit	Balance
(B)	20__ Oct.	4		G8	(A) 500		500
				(C)			

Notice that the Balance column of the General Ledger is not labeled Debit or Credit. This column always represents the normal balance of the account. In the example above, the normal balance of the Cash account is Debit. The General Ledger indicates that Cash has a $300 debit balance.

CROSS REFERENCING

It is now possible to tie together quickly the debit and credit for each transaction. Posting references refer to each other—the journal to the account number (i.e., 11, 53), the account to the journal page number (i.e., G8). This is called CROSS REFERENCING. It makes the work of checking the records much simpler.

The bookkeeping process starts with the source document for a transaction. A journal entry is then recorded in the General Journal. The entry is posted to ledger accounts in the General Ledger.

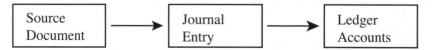

Trial Balance

When all journalizing and posting has been completed at the end of the month, the bookkeeping clerk checks the accuracy of that work. A listing is made of all ledger accounts and their balances: this is called a TRIAL BALANCE.

In preparing a trial balance, the following steps are taken:

(1) Find the balance of each account. This is the final amount in the Balance Column of the General Ledger.

(2) Accounts will normally have balances (debit or credit) on their *increase* sides—assets are debits, liabilities are credits, owner's equity (capital) is a credit, revenue is a credit, and expenses are debits.

Account No. 16
Supplies

Date		Explanation	PR	Debit	Credit	Balance
20__						
Oct.	2		G5	100		100
	14		G7	50		150
	28		G9		20	130
	30		G10	35		165

Above is a typical account showing a debit balance of $165.

(3) Start the trial balance with a heading to answer the questions WHO, WHAT, and WHEN. List the name of the company, the type of report, and the date of the report.

(4) List all accounts by name in their numerical order. Each account balance is placed in either the debit or credit column (see page 39).

(5) Finally, total each column. If all work is done correctly, the totals should be equal. Once again, debits equal credits. The trial balance is said to be IN BALANCE. Double-rule the totals to show that the work has been completed and no further adding or subtracting will be done.

Following is a ledger of simple T-account balances:

Cash	Equipment	Supplies
2500	5000	165

Accounts Payable	Van Loc, Capital	Rent Income
1115	5000	2000

Advertising Expense	Salary Expense
50	400

At the end of the month (October 31) the bookkeeping clerk will prepare a trial balance of the general ledger, following the five steps listed on page 38.

Van Loc Company

Trial Balance

October 31, 20__

Account Title	Debit	Credit
Cash	2500 00	
Equipment	5000 00	
Supplies	165 00	
Accounts Payable		1115 00
Van Loc, Capital		5000 00
Rent Income		2000 00
Advertising Expense	50 00	
Salary Expense	400 00	
Totals	8115 00	8115 00

YOU SHOULD REMEMBER

- Account *balances* normally reflect the side on which *the account increases*.
- A trial balance *proves* the *equality of debits and credits in the ledger.*

LOCATING TRIAL BALANCE ERRORS

A trial balance taken at the time interval desired—end of month, fiscal period, year—is a test of the equality of the debit and credit account balances in the ledger. If, however, a trial balance is OUT OF BALANCE, the following steps—in reverse order—should be taken to determine the reason(s).

Source
Document

↓

Journal

↓

Ledger

↓

Trial
Balance

(1) Re-add the columns of the trial balance; perhaps they were totaled incorrectly.

(2) Examine each account balance in the trial balance, and compare these account balances to the ledger account balances. Perhaps they were carried forward incorrectly, or perhaps an account was omitted, listed twice, or placed in the wrong amount column of the trial balance (reversing a debit or a credit).

(3) Check the ledger accounts to verify each account balance.

(4) If an error is not located at this point, compare each entry in the account with the original debit and credit recorded in the journal entry.

When an error is discovered in the ledger, neatly cross out the incorrect entry and write the correction above it. Never erase ink amounts or mark through an error in any way that causes the first figure to be altered. This could cause legal problems, inasmuch as bookkeeping/accounting records are legal documents.

ERRORS THAT THE TRIAL BALANCE DOES NOT REVEAL

Not all errors show up in a trial balance. The following errors do not affect the equality of debits and credits in the ledger:

(1) Omitting an entire entry.

(2) Posting to an incorrect account—a debit to another debit, a credit to another credit.

(3) Using an incorrect amount in a journal entry and posting that amount to ledger accounts.

(4) Recording a transaction twice.

KNOW YOUR VOCABULARY

- Balance
- Cross referencing
- Footings
- In balance
- Posting
- Trial balance

QUESTIONS

1. What steps are followed in posting journal entries?

2. a) What does the journal posting refer to?
   b) What does the account posting refer to?

3. A bookkeeping clerk resumes his/her posting work after returning from lunch. How will he/she know where to resume?

4. What does a trial balance that is "in balance" prove?

5. What is the order in which work will be checked to find an error in the trial balance?

6. What errors will cause a trial balance to be out of balance?

7. What errors can be made that will not cause a trial balance to be out of balance?

PROBLEMS

4-1 Post the four transactions from the General Journal to the General Ledger on page 43. After each account is posted, enter the account number in the posting reference column of the General Journal.

GENERAL JOURNAL   Page 6

Date		Accounts	PR	Debit	Credit
20__ Oct.	1	Equipment		1000 00	
		Accounts Payable–Landers Mfg. Co.			1000 00
		5 Motors, Voucher No. 31			
	10	Cash		250 00	
		Service Income			250 00
		Receipts Nos. 1–35, to date			
	18	L.D. Berger, Drawing		50 00	
		Cash			50 00
		Withdrawal, Personal Use,			
		Check No. 57			
	25	Accounts Payable–Landers Mfg. Company		25 00	
		Cash			25 00
		Partial Payment, Check No. 58			

Account No. 11
Cash

Date	Explanation	PR	Debit	Credit	Balance
20__					

Account No. 12
Equipment

Date	Explanation	PR	Debit	Credit	Balance
20__					

Account No. 21
Accounts Payable

Date	Explanation	PR	Debit	Credit	Balance
20__					

Account No. 32
Berger, Drawing

Date	Explanation	PR	Debit	Credit	Balance
20__					

Account No. 41
Service Income

Date	Explanation	PR	Debit	Credit	Balance
20__					

4-2 Below, in a T-account form, is the general ledger for Alan Korn, who operates a computer consulting firm:

Cash	No. 11		Equipment	No. 12
1500	100		3500	
750	50		465	
495	75			
	500		**Supplies**	**No. 13**
			60	
Accounts Payable	**No. 21**			
75	2000		**Alan Korn, Drawing**	**No. 32**
	465		500	
Alan Korn, Capital	**No. 31**		**Advertising Expense**	**No. 51**
	3060		100	
Services Income	**No. 41**		**Utilities Expense**	**No. 52**
	750		50	
	495			

(1) Pencil-foot the ledger to find the balance of each account. First, total each column. Then subtract the smaller total from the larger total. Write your answer under the larger total.

(2) Prepare a trial balance, using today's date.

4-3 Anita Schaffer runs knitting and sewing classes from her home. Last month she completed the following transactions:

October 2	Bought class supplies for cash, $125
7	Received class fees, $200
11	Made a $50 payment to Jessup Bank due on loan
21	Received class fees, $240
27	Paid $65 for miscellaneous expenses
31	Withdrew $300 for personal use

(1) Record the transactions above in Schaffer's journal.

(2) Post the journal entries to Schaffer's ledger accounts.

(3) Prepare a trial balance, dated October 31, 20___.

(1) *GENERAL JOURNAL* *Page 3*

Date	Account Title	PR	Debit	Credit

4-3 (2)

Account No. 11
Cash

Date	Explanation	PR	Debit	Credit	Balance
20__ Oct. 1	Balance	✓			1375

Account No. 12
Equipment

Date	Explanation	PR	Debit	Credit	Balance
20__ Oct. 1	Balance	✓			1642.50

Account No. 13
Supplies

Date	Explanation	PR	Debit	Credit	Balance
20__ Oct. 1	Balance	✓			230

Account No. 21
Note Payable

Date	Explanation	PR	Debit	Credit	Balance
20__ Oct. 1	Balance	✓			875

Account No. 31
Anita Schaffer, Capital

Date	Explanation	PR	Debit	Credit	Balance
20__ Oct. 1	Balance	✓			2372.50

Account No. 32
Anita Schaffer, Drawing

Date	Explanation	PR	Debit	Credit	Balance

Account No. 41
Fee Income

Date	Explanation	PR	Debit	Credit	Balance

Account No. 51
Miscellaneous Expense

Date	Explanation	PR	Debit	Credit	Balance

(3) _____

_____

_____

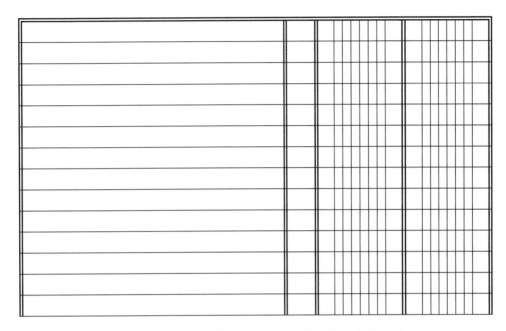

4-4 T. R. Price is a carpenter who receives a commission for odd jobs in his neighborhood. His bookkeeping records indicate the following balances (shown in T-account form):

Cash 11		Equipment 12		Truck 13	
2645		1500		7500	

Accounts Payable 21		T. R. Price, Capital 31		T. R. Price, Drawing 32	
	550		10570	500	

Commissions Income 41		Advertising Expense 51		Miscellaneous Expense 52	
	1650	100		50	

Rent Expense 53		Salary Expense 54	
175		300	

Prepare a trial balance for the month ended November 30, 20__.

4-5 Below is a trial balance for Ann Danziger; however, it contains an error.

Danziger Designs

Trial Balance

September 30, 20__

Cash	11	176250	
Accounts Receivable	12	73890	
Equipment	13	260500	
Supplies	14	39500	
Accounts Payable	21	60000	
Ann Danziger, Capital	31		425140
Ann Danziger, Drawing	32	80000	
Fees Income	41		240000
Advertising Expense	51	16000	
Insurance Expense	52	4000	
Materials Expense	53	10000	
Rent Expense	54	25000	
Salary Expense	55	40000	

(1) Find the error and move the amount from one column to the other, thus correcting the trial balance.

(2) Total the trial balance.

4-6 Rebecca Gayle operates a message delivery service. Her trial balance for the month ended October 31, 20__, is shown below:

Gayle's Reliable Service

Trial Balance

October 31, 20__

		Debit	Credit
Cash	11	760 00	
Accounts Receivable	12	142 50	
Automobile	13	9200 00	
Supplies	14	350 00	
Note Payable	21		3600 00
Rebecca Gayle, Capital	31		6302 00
Rebecca Gayle, Drawing	32	600 00	
Service Income	41	1875 50	
Advertising Expense	51	200 00	
Auto Expense	52	400 00	
Miscellaneous Expense	53	50 00	
Telephone Expense	54	75 00	

(1) Find the error and move the amount from one column to the other, thus correcting the trial balance.

THINK IT OVER

1. Dina Fowler has prepared a trial balance for her business. It is not in balance. She asks you where she should review her bookkeeping work, in order to find the reason. What suggestions will you make?

2. Ira Jacobs has prepared a trial balance that is in balance. On reviewing his work however, he discovers that he omitted one entry for a payment of $50 for an expense. Why did this error, or omission, not affect the equality of debits and credits in his ledger?

3. Can you suggest other kinds of errors that might *not* cause a trial balance to be "out of balance"?

4. Damien Spyridon's trial balance is not in balance. He checks his work and finds two errors. An expense account with a $100 balance was listed on the trial balance as a credit. The other error is found when he checks his posting. A journal entry amount was $54; he posted the debit as $45. Why did the trial balance columns differ by $209?

Adjusting Entries

WORDS TO REMEMBER

- **Adjusting Entry** an entry made at the *end of a fiscal period* to bring *an account balance up to date*
- **Prepaid Expenses** expenses that are paid more than one month in advance.

SECTIONS IN THIS CHAPTER

- Adjustments to Entries
- Posting to the General Ledger

Up to this point, the bookkeeping/accounting cycle has followed these steps:

(1) A business transaction occurs, resulting in a source document—an invoice (sales and purchases), a check, a debit or credit memorandum, and so on.

(2) The transaction is journalized.

(3) The journal entry is posted to ledger accounts.

(4) A trial balance is prepared.

Adjustments to Entries

The next step in the cycle is to prepare a type of journal entry called an adjusting entry. These entries are necessary to ensure that all of the accounts accurately reflect the financial position of the business. Some changes in account balances have not been recorded in the journals, and therefore not posted to accounts. It is necessary to bring them up to date. This is accomplished by entering ADJUSTMENTS in the general journal and posting these adjusting entries to the general ledger. Several common types of adjustments are described below.

SUPPLIES

The trial balance lists the SUPPLIES account at an amount which includes its beginning balance plus any supplies acquired during the fiscal period. The fact that some of these supplies may have been used during the fiscal period has not been recorded. Therefore, a supplies inventory is taken to determine the value on hand at the end of the fiscal period. To find the *amount used* during that time, the ending inventory is subtracted from the account balance. The *difference is the expense* for supplies. The adjusting entry *debits Supplies Expense* and *credits Supplies* for that *difference*.

It is important to understand the purpose of both the Supplies account and the Supplies Expense account. The Supplies account is an asset that reports the amount of supplies the business has on hand. Supplies Expense is an expense account that reports the amount of supplies that was used by the business during a period of time (usually one month).

PREPAID EXPENSES

Prepaid Expense is a term used for expenses that are paid more than one month in advance. Although these accounts have the word "expense" in the title, they are actually asset accounts. Examples of commonly used prepaid expenses are Prepaid Insurance and Prepaid Rent. If a business pays for only one-month's worth of insurance, it would record that as Insurance Expense. However, if the business paid for two or more months of insurance at one time, it would record that payment as Prepaid Insurance. See illustration below.

| 10/1 | Insurance Expense | $100 | |
| | Cash | | $100 |

To record payment of insurance at a cost of $100 per month.

| 10/1 | Prepaid Insurance | $600 | |
| | Cash | | $600 |

To record payment of 6 months of insurance at a cost of $100 per month.
($100 × 6 = $600)

In the second entry above, the business has paid $600 for 6 months of insurance. At the end of each month, it is necessary to recognize the use of one month of insurance by reducing the value of the asset account by $100. This is accomplished with the adjusting journal entry below.

| 10/31 | Insurance Expense | $100 | |
| | Prepaid Insurance | | $100 |

This entry increases the expense account and reduces the asset account for the amount of insurance that was used up during the month. After this entry is posted to the ledger, the Prepaid Insurance account is reduced from $600 to $500. A similar adjusting entry would be recorded and posted at the end of each of the following 5 months, reducing the Prepaid Insurance account by $100 each time until it reaches a value of zero at the end of the 6 month period.

You may be wondering why it is necessary to create a prepaid expense account in this situation, rather than just recording the entire payment of $600 to Insurance Expense. In the next chapter, you will learn that journal entries are the basis for creating financial statements. These statements report the financial position of the business at a point in time. If the business owner wants to know how the business has performed financially during the month, it is reasonable to report only one-month's expenses. This approach follows the matching principle, since the total revenue is for only one month as well.

UNEARNED REVENUES

In some cases, a business will receive money in advance for services that will be provided in the future. This situation creates a liability—an obligation to provide those services at a later date. Consider an attorney who receives a payment of $500 from a client before any services are provided. Since revenues are recorded when they are earned, this receipt cannot be treated as income at this time. The attorney would record the receipt of $500 in cash as follows:

| 10/7 | Cash | $500 | |
| | Unearned Fees | | $500 |

The Cash account has increased, reflecting receipt of $500. A liability account (Unearned Fees) has been created to recognize the obligation to provide legal services valued at $500.

Assume that during October, the attorney draws up a will for his client and completes the agreed upon services. At the end of the month, the obligation has been satisfied and a liability no longer exists. The adjusting entry will remove the liability and record the revenue that is earned during October.

| 10/31 | Unearned Fees | $500 | |
| | Legal Fees Earned | | $500 |

After this journal entry is posted to the ledger, the Unearned Fees account will have a zero balance because the obligation has been satisfied. Legal Fees Earned, a revenue account, reflects the income that is earned during October.

ACCRUED REVENUES

Some adjusting entries are necessary because of timing issues. In accounting, to accrue means to accumulate. Revenues must be recorded in the proper period. Recall that most journal entries are prepared based on source documents. In the case of revenues, the business prepares an invoice or bill that describes the transaction. The bookkeeper then records the revenue using information on the invoice. In many businesses, there is a delay between the date of sale and the date the invoice is prepared.

Assume that Joe Smith, Attorney, provides legal services ($400) on account to his client. These services occur on Friday, October 30. Joe's bookkeeper creates an invoice on Monday, November 2, and mails it to the client. Both the revenue recognition principle and the matching principle require the revenue to be recorded in the month of October since that is when it was earned. Without an adjustment, the invoice would prompt the bookkeeper to record the revenue in November. The resulting journal entry is the same. The only difference is in the date applied to the entry.

| 10/31 | Accounts Receivable | $400 | |
| | Legal Fees Earned | | $400 |

To record legal fees provided to a client on account.

ACCRUED EXPENSES

A similar type of adjustment is called an accrued expense. As in the case of revenues, expenses must also be recorded in the proper period. The bookkeeper generally uses a bill received from a vendor (supplier) to generate the journal entry for an expense. This process can create timing issues as well.

Consider the electric bill as an example. Electricity is used during October, but the bill will probably arrive in November. The cost of the electricity must be recorded in

October, since that is when the expense was incurred. If the amount of the electric bill is about the same each month, then no adjustment is necessary. The bookkeeper just ensures that a month of electric expense is recorded.

However, if the bill varies significantly from month to month, or if the expense is not a regularly occurring one, it is important to create an adjusting entry to record the correct amount of expense in the related period. Note that the date of the entry below is October 31, even though the bill may not be received until some time in November. Depending on the type of expense and the amount involved, the bookkeeper may be able to estimate an appropriate amount. If the amount is difficult to estimate, it may be necessary to call the vendor and ask for a projected dollar amount. The adjusting entry to record electric usage for October would be:

10/31	Utilities Expense	$150	
	Accounts Payable		$150

To record electricity costs for October.

ACCRUED SALARIES

Employee salaries are a unique type of accrued expense. Although employees may be paid by the week, the salary expense must be recorded for the calendar month. Adjustments are required when the end of the work week does not coincide with the end of the month.

For example, assume that employees are paid every Friday. For October, the final payday occurs on Friday, October 27. The following week, employees continue to work Monday–Friday. Monday is October 30, and Tuesday is October 31. If an employee is paid $200/week or $40/day, this must be prorated for journalizing purposes. Earnings for Monday and Tuesday, October 30 & 31, amounting to $80 (40 × 2), are recorded in October. Earnings for Wednesday–Friday, November 1–3, amounting to $120 ($40 × 3), are recorded in November. From the employee's perspective, they receive $200 for the week. It is the bookkeeper's responsibility to ensure that the earnings are journalized correctly. Ignoring any deductions for taxes and so on, the adjusting entry for October would be:

10/31	Salaries Expense	$80	
	Salaries Payable		$80

To record salaries for October 30 & 31

Another entry would be recorded in November for the entire week's salary as follows:

11/3	Salaries Payable	$80	
	Salaries Expense	$120	
	Cash		$200

To record payment of employee salaries.

The November 3 entry eliminates the salaries payable liability account. A total of $200 has been debited to salaries expense; $80 on October 31 and $120 on November 3.

Posting to the General Ledger

Adjusting entries are first recorded in the general journal. These ADJUSTING ENTRIES reflected the changes that had taken place but had not been recorded in the actual accounts. *General ledger accounts* must now be brought up to date at the end of the fiscal period so that these changes become part of the permanent bookkeeping/accounting records.

The illustration below shows an adjusting entry *posted* to general ledger accounts.

GENERAL JOURNAL   *Page 4*

Date			PR	Dr.	Cr.
20__					
		Adjusting Entries			
Dec.	31	*Supplies Expenses*	515	95000	
		Supplies	116		95000

Supplies   *No. 116*

Date			PR	Dr.	Cr.	Balance
20__						
Jan.	1	*Balance*	✓			50000
May.	15		CP3	60000		110000
Nov.	3		CP8	29000		139000
Dec.	31	*Adjustment*	G4		95000	44000

Supplies Expense   *No. 515*

Date			PR	Dr.	Cr.	Balance
20__ Dec.	31	Adjustment	G4	95000		95000

The ledger Posting Reference (PR) column indicates postings from general journal page 4 (G4). These accounts—Supplies, and Supplies Expense—are now up to date.

YOU SHOULD REMEMBER

- Adjusting entries are dated on the last day of the fiscal period.
- The cash account is not used in any of these adjusting entries.
- Adjustments are simple journal entries, with only one debit and one credit.
- Prepaid expenses *are assets when first acquired*, but become expenses as they are used, thus requiring an adjustment to record this change.

KNOW YOUR VOCABULARY

- Accrued Expenses
- Accrued Revenues
- Adjustments (adjusting entries)
- Merchandise inventory
- Prepaid assets
- Unearned Revenue

QUESTIONS

1. What are the two accounting principles linked to adjusting entries?

2. What does the amount of the supplies adjustment represent?

3. Why do prepaid expenses have to be adjusted at the end of a fiscal period?

PROBLEMS

5-1 Daniel Green's general ledger account balances are given below:

Cash	$1,200
Accounts Receivable	2,500
Equipment	6,000
Supplies	400
Prepaid Insurance	300
Accounts Payable	1,800
Daniel Green, Capital	14,200 ($12,200 plus additional $2,000 investment)
Daniel Green, Drawing	$1,500
Legal Fees Earned	6,500
Miscellaneous Expense	100
Rent Expense	1,200
Salary Expense	1,500
Supplies Expense	?

Complete the journal on page 59 for the month ended June 30, using the following information for adjustments.

1. Supplies on hand $300

2. Six months of insurance premiums were paid on June 1

3. Accrued salaries amounted to $500

5–1

5-2 Timothy Sullivan's general ledger is given on pages 61–63.

(a) Complete the general journal below using the following additional information to record adjustments for the month of January.

   1. Supplies on hand $205

   2. Insurance costs $50 per month

   3. Accrued legal fees earned are $500

   4. Accrued advertising costs are $250

(b) Post your journal entries to the ledger.

5–2(a) _____ *Page 6*

Cash   *No. 11*

Date			PR	Dr.	Cr.	Balance
20__ Jan.	1	Balance	✓			1500 00
	31		G3	3650 00		5150 00
	31		G3		1790 00	3360 00

Accounts Receivable   *No. 12*

Date			PR	Dr.	Cr.	Balance
20__ Jan.	1	Balance	✓			500 00
	31		G3	3200 00		3700 00
	31		G3		150 00	3550 00
	31		G3		35 00	3515 00

Supplies   *No. 14*

Date			PR	Dr.	Cr.	Balance
20__ Jan.	1	Balance	✓			275 00
	3		G1	50 00		325 00

Prepaid Insurance   *No. 15*

Date			PR	Dr.	Cr.	Balance
20__ Jan.	1	Balance	✓			300 00

Accounts Payable   *No. 21*

Date			PR	Dr.	Cr.	Balance
20__ Jan.	1	Balance	✓			1000 00
	31		G3		1200 00	2200 00
	31		G3	400 00		1800 00

Timothy Sullivan, Capital   *No. 31*

Date			PR	Dr.	Cr.	Balance
20__ Jan.	1	Balance	✓			5375 00
	10		G2		2500 00	7875 00

Timothy Sullivan, Drawing   *No. 32*

Date			PR	Dr.	Cr.	Balance
20__ Jan.	15	Balance	G2	150 00		150 00
	30		G3	150 00		300 00

Legal Fees Earned   *No. 41*

Date			PR	Dr.	Cr.	Balance
20__ Jan.	31		G3		3200 00	3200 00
	31		G3		1000 00	4200 00

Advertising Expense   No. 51

Date			PR	Dr.	Cr.	Balance
20__ Jan.	3		G1	10000		10000

Insurance Expense   No. 52

Date			PR	Dr.	Cr.	Balance

Miscellaneous Expense   No. 53

Date			PR	Dr.	Cr.	Balance
20__ Jan.	12		G2	2500		2500
	27		G3	1500		4000

Rent Expense   No. 54

Date			PR	Dr.	Cr.	Balance
20__ Jan.	2		G1	40000		40000

Supplies Expense   No. 55

Date			PR	Dr.	Cr.	Balance

Financial Statements

WORDS TO REMEMBER

- **Account Form** the arrangement of a *balance sheet*, with *assets* listed on *the left side*, *liabilities* and *owner's equity on the right side*
- **Articles of Partnership** the *written agreement* establishing a partnership
- **Balance Sheet** a financial statement that lists all *assets owned* and all *claims against assets*, thus revealing one's *financial condition*
- **Creditor** one to whom a debt is *owed*
- **Fiscal Period** the *length of time* covered by the financial statements
- **Income Statement** a financial statement listing all revenue and expenses for a fiscal period, leading to the net income or net loss; a statement that describes the operations of a business over a period of time (fiscal period)
- **Owner's Equity Statement** a financial statement that shows how owner's equity has changed during a fiscal period

SECTIONS IN THIS CHAPTER

- To Summarize a Business
- Income Statement
- Owner's Equity Statement
- Balance Sheet

To Summarize a Business

At the end of each fiscal period, financial statements are prepared to summarize the operations of a business. Usually, financial statements are prepared at the end of a definite period of time—the FISCAL PERIOD. This can be monthly, quarterly, semi-monthly, or annually. A 12-month fiscal period, however, need not coincide with the 12 calendar months of the year. A fiscal year could run from July 1 to the following June 30, or from April 1 to the following March 31.

Information from the financial statements allows the owner(s) to see how profitable (or unprofitable) the business has been, to compare one fiscal period with prior periods, and to determine future courses of action. In addition, this information may be requested by banks, and by the Internal Revenue Service if tax returns are examined. Financial statements are prepared after the adjusting trial balance has been completed. There are four major financial statements: income statement, owner's equity statement, balance sheet, and cash flow statement. The first three are discussed here.

Income Statement

An INCOME STATEMENT shows the results of operations for a business during a fiscal period. It is prepared from information on the adjusted trial balance.

The income statement for Van Loc Company appears below:

Van Loc Company

Income Statement

For the Month Ended October 31, 20__

Revenue:				
Rent Income				2 0 0 00
Expenses:				
Advertising Expense		1 5 0 00		
Salary Expense		4 0 0 00		
Total Expense				5 5 0 00
Net Income				1 4 5 0 00

The customary three-line heading indicates the answers to WHO, WHAT, and WHEN. The statement is divided into three parts.

1. A *revenue* section, listing all operating income earned during the fiscal period

2. The *expenses* section, listing all operating expenses for the fiscal period (overhead).

3. The *net income*, which is the difference between total revenues and total expenses

Total Revenues – Total Expenses = Net Income (or Net Loss)

If expenses are greater than revenue, the difference (revenue subtracted from expenses) is identified as a net loss. Note that the money column on the left is used to list more than one item; the money column on the right is for totals (or a single item) and the results of the business operations for the fiscal period—net income or net loss. Double lines are ruled through both money columns to show a completed statement. An income statement for a business owned by a single owner does not differ from one for a business owned by two or more people (a partnership).

Owner's Equity Statement

The next financial statement to be prepared is the Owner's Equity Statement. It shows how owner's equity has changed during a fiscal period. The statement starts with the *beginning* capital account balance. Any changes that occur are then listed. Possible changes in owner's equity are:

Increases	Decreases
(1) additional investments	(1) withdrawals
(2) net income for period	(2) net loss for period

Van Loc's owner's equity statement is a simple one; only one item is involved.

Van Loc Company

Owner's Equity Statement

For the Month Ended October 31, 20__

Beginning Capital Balance, Oct. 1, 20__		5 1 5 0 00
Plus: Net Income		1 4 5 0 00
Ending Capital, Oct. 31, 20__		6 6 0 0 00

Following are illustrations of owner's equity statements with more changes (headings are omitted here):

Beginning Capital, Sept. 1, 20__			7500 00
Plus: Additional Investment		1000 00	
Net Income		2500 00	
		3500 00	
Less: Withdrawals		1500 00	
Net Increase in Capital			2000 00
Ending Capital, Sept. 30, 20__			9500 00

With decreases less than increases, there is a *net increase* in capital. Always verify whichever one there is before writing the words "Net Increase" or "Net Decrease." (If withdrawals are greater than any additional investment, there may still be a net decrease—assuming a net income that does not make up the difference.)

Beginning Capital, Nov. 1, 201_			12500 00
Plus: Additional Investment			3000 00
Less: Withdrawals		1500 00	
Net Loss		2000 00	
Decrease in Capital			3500 00
Ending Capital, Nov. 30, 201_			12000 00

OWNER'S EQUITY STATEMENT FOR A PARTNERSHIP

A partnership is a business with two or more owners. The OWNER'S EQUITY STATEMENT shows how each partner's owner's equity changed during the fiscal period.

There must be an agreement as to how partners are to share any net income or net loss. If Fields and Ross, two partners, share a net income of $32,260 equally, each partner would receive $16,130 (one half of $32,260). If partners share in any other way, this must be clearly stated in the ARTICLES OF PARTNERSHIP, the written agreement establishing the business. Assume, in the case of Fields and Ross, that the agreement provides for the partners to share income and losses *in the ratio* of 3 to 2 (3:2). This means that Fields would receive three fifths ($\frac{3}{5}$) or 60%, and Ross two fifths ($\frac{2}{5}$) or 40%, of any net income or any net loss.

Field's share of the net income is, therefore, $19,356 ($\frac{3}{5}$ or 60% of $32,260), and Ross's share is $12,904 ($\frac{2}{5}$ or 40% of $32,260).

Fields and Ross

Owner's Equity Statement

For Year Ended December 31, 20___

A. G. Fields:			
Beginning Capital, Jan.1		11 595 00	
Plus: 3/5 of Net Income	19 356 00		
Less: Withdrawals	12 000 00		
Net Increase in Capital		7 356 00	
Ending Capital, Dec.31			18 951 00
B. W. Ross:			
Beginning Capital, Jan. 1		10 610 00	
Plus: Additional Investment	2 000 00		
2/5 of Net Income	12 904 00		
Increase in Capital	14 904 00		
Less: Withdrawals	12 000 00		
Net Increase in Capital		2 904 00	
Ending Capital, Dec. 31			13 514 00
Total Owner's Equity, Dec. 31			32 465 00

Examine the following owner's equity statement for Lois Berlowitz, who had a loss for the fiscal period:

Lois Berlowitz			
Owner's Equity Statement			
For Six Months Ended June 30, 20__			

Beginning Capital, Jan. 1			28765 00
Additional Investment			2500 00
			31265 00
Less: Net Loss		5200 00	
Withdrawals		6000 00	
Total Decrease in Capital			11200 00
Ending Capital, June 30			20065 00

Balance Sheet

The next financial statement to be prepared is a BALANCE SHEET. It shows the financial condition of a business at the end of the fiscal period.

When all three elements of bookkeeping—assets, liabilities, and owner's equity—are examined together, they appear in the form of a BALANCE SHEET.

PURPOSE, FORM, AND CONTENT

A balance sheet is a financial statement or business form that lists, as of a certain date, all assets owned and all claims against these assets. These claims are held by CREDITORS, to whom money is owed, and the owners themselves, in the form of their owner's equity. When arranged in this way, it is easy to see that the fundamental bookkeeping equation again holds true:

$$A = L + OE$$

A bookkeeper or accounting clerk prepared a very simple balance sheet for Van Loc Company on October 31 of the current year.

The capital *at the end of the fiscal period* is the ending balance found on the owner's equity statement shown previously.

Van Loc Company

Balance Sheet

October 31, 20__

Assets		Liabilities and Owner's Equity	
Cash	2500 00	Liabilities	
Equipment	5000 00	Accounts Payable	1200 00
Supplies	300 00	Owner's Equity	
Total Assets	7800 00	Van Loc Cap., Oct. 31	6600 00
		Total Liab. & O.E.	7800 00

Compare Van Loc's capital with the amount listed on his owner's equity statement, page 67. These two items will always agree.

The form presented on page 72 is the REPORT FORM balance sheet, listing items (assets, liabilities, and owner's equity) vertically, one under the other. Notice, however, that the fundamental bookkeeping/accounting equation is maintained and is emphasized by double-ruling *total assets* and *total liabilities plus owners' equity*. This balance sheet is for a partnership. The only change is that there are two capital accounts.

Fields and Ross

Balance Sheet

December 31, 20__

Assets			
Cash		2 25 0 00	
Accounts Receivable		3 17 5 00	
Equipment		15 00 0 00	
Supplies		4 4 0 00	
Total Assets			20 86 5 00
Liabilities			
Accounts Payable			2 05 0 00
Owner's Equity			
A. G. Fields, Capital		7 35 1 00	
B. W. Ross, Capital		11 46 4 00	
Total Owner's Equity			18 81 5 00
Total Liabilities and Owners' Equity			20 86 5 00

A somewhat more elaborate balance sheet for Thomas Morales's landscaping business is shown below:

Evergreen Landscaping Service

Balance Sheet

September 30, 20__

Assets		Liabilities and Owner's Equity	
Cash	7 85 0 00	Liabilities	
Truck	11 00 0 00	Accounts Payable	1 34 5 00
Haulaway Trailer	1 50 0 00	Notes Payable	7 70 0 00
Accounts Receivable	3 60 0 00	Total Liabilities	9 04 5 00
Equipment	3 32 0 00	Owner's Equity	
Office Furniture	75 0 00	Thomas Morales, Capital	19 72 0 00
Supplies	74 5 00	Total Liabilities &	
Total Assets	28 76 5 00	Owner's Equity	28 76 5 00

This balance sheet shows the FINANCIAL CONDITION of Morales's business on the specified date. When this form is arranged with two sides—assets on the left, liabilities and owner's equity on the right—it is called an ACCOUNT FORM balance sheet.

Note the following details carefully:

1. The heading consists of "answers" to the questions WHO, WHAT, and WHEN.

2. The account form lists assets on the left side, liabilities and owner's equity on the right side.

3. The sum of all assets is listed below the last one and identified as "Total Assets."

4. The sum of all liabilities is listed below the last one and identified as "Total Liabilities."

5. The sum of total liabilities and capital is listed on the *same line level* as the total assets and identified as "Total Liabilities and Owner's Equity" or with acceptable abbreviations.

6. The final total dollar amounts on both sides are double ruled.

7. The dollar symbol, comma, and decimal point are not used in any bookkeeping form or statement.

(Single ruled lines indicate an addition or subtraction. Double ruled lines indicate the end of the work.)

FUNDAMENTAL BOOKKEEPING EQUATION

The fundamental bookkeeping equation is clearly seen on each balance sheet. The dollar value of total assets on the left side equals the dollar value of the creditors' claims (liabilities) plus capital (owner's equity) on the right side.

YOU SHOULD REMEMBER

- Three items in a statement heading explain WHO, WHAT, and WHEN.
- Assets *equal liabilities plus owner's equity*, or
- Assets *minus liabilities equal owner's equity*.
- When *revenue is greater than expenses* there is a *net income*.
- When *expenses are greater than revenue* there is a net loss.
- Owner's equity is *increased* by:
  - additional investments and
  - net income.
- Owner's equity is *decreased* by:
  - withdrawals by the owner and
  - net loss.

KNOW YOUR VOCABULARY

Use each of the following words or terms in a statement relating to bookkeeping/accounting:

- Account form
- Articles of Partnership
- Balance sheet
- Claims against assets
- Creditor
- Financial condition
- Fiscal period
- Income Statement
- Owner's Equity Statement

QUESTIONS

1. What three questions are answered in the heading of a balance sheet?

2. How many days are there in each month?

3. What is the last day of a quarterly fiscal period beginning on July 1? On January 1? On October 1?

4. What determines that a balance sheet is "in balance"?

5. How can owner's equity be found if total assets and total liabilities are known?

6. In what order should statements be prepared?

7. What are the causes for an increase in owner's equity?

8. What are the causes for a decrease in owner's equity?

9. How are the dates indicated in the "when" part of each statement's heading?

10. What information is shown on each of the following?

    a) An income statement.
    b) An owner's equity statement.
    c) A balance sheet.

11. What determines whether there is a net income or a net loss for a fiscal period?

12. How does a report form balance sheet differ from an account form balance sheet?

PROBLEMS

6-1 Name the section of a balance sheet—Assets, Liabilities, or Owner's Equity—in which each of the following items should be located:

Example: Machinery

1. Supplies	1.	
2. Amounts owed to creditors	2.	
3. Tools	3.	
4. Bank loan	4.	
5. Office equipment	5.	
6. Checking account balance	6.	
7. Amount due from customer	7.	
8. Owner's financial claim	8.	
9. Furniture	9.	
10. Capital	10.	

Balance Sheet

Left Side	Right Side
Asset	

6-2   On August 31 of the current year, the following assets and liabilities were listed by Maria Lopez, owner of Maria's Beauty Salon:

Assets:	Cash	$1,750
	Furniture and Fixtures	8,900
	Beauty Supplies	600
Liabilities:	Accounts Payable	2,775

Prepare a balance sheet for Maria's Beauty Salon on the date indicated. Use the form in this chapter (page 71) for your model.

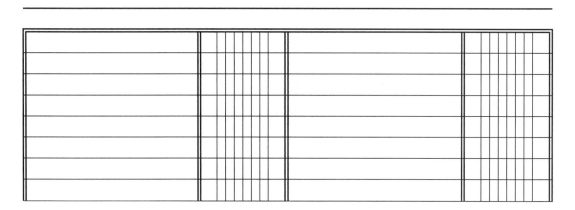

6-3   Lady Cake Bake Shoppe reports the following assets and liabilities on July 31 of the current year.

Assets:	Cash	$1,250.00
	Building	68,500.00
	Bakery Equipment	26,200.00
	Furniture and Fixtures	6,300.00
	Supplies	1,800.00
Liabilities:	Note Payable	23,575.00
	Accounts Payable	5,350.00

Prepare a balance sheet for the Lady Cake Bake Shoppe on the date indicated. Gustave Mueller is the owner.

_____

_____

_____

6-4   Using the completed trial balance in Problem 4-4 for T. R. Price, complete the following:

a)   An income statement.

b)   An owner's equity statement

c)   A balance sheet. (Enter the liabilities and owner's equity total on the same line level with the assets total before double ruling.)

a)   _____

_____

b)

c)

6-5 Using the corrected trial balance in Problem 4-5 for Danziger Designs, complete the following:

   a) An income statement.

   b) An owner's equity statement.

   c) A balance sheet. (Enter the liabilities and owner's equity total on the same line level with the assets total before double ruling.)

a) _____

b) _____

c) _____

6-6 Using the corrected trial balance in Problem 4-6 for Rebecca Gayle, complete the following:

a) An income statement.

b) An owner's equity statement.

c) A balance sheet. (Enter the liabilities and owner's equity total on the same line level with the assets total before double ruling.)

a) _____

b) _____

c) _____

_____

6-7 Comprehensive Problem

This problem will review all of the steps in the bookkeeping cycle that you have learned so far.

Complete each section in the order presented.

a) Journalize the following transactions in the general journal provided.

7/1   Sheila Brown invested $8,000 to start her business, Brown Consulting.

7/2   Sheila paid six month's rent in advance ($3,600) to secure her office space.

7/2   The business purchased $200 of office supplies on account.

7/5   The business purchased $800 of equipment and $500 of furniture for cash.

7/7   Sheila provided $1200 of design services for a client on credit.

7/12   Sheila provided an additional $400 of design services for a client and received payment in cash.

7/20   Paid for the office supplies purchased on 7/2.

7/23   The client paid for $600 of the services provided on 7/7.

7/25   Sheila paid $200 for advertising.

7/28   Sheila received $500 from a client for design services to be performed next month.

7/29   The client paid the balance due on the 7/7 transaction.

b) Post your journal entries to the general ledger.

c) Prepare a trial balance.

d) Journalize and post these adjusting entries:

7/31 $75 of office supplies have been used.

7/31 $300 of design services provided on 7/31 have not yet been billed.

7/31   Sheila knows that a telephone bill of $50 for July services is in the mail.

7/31   One month's rent has expired (been used up).

e) Prepare an adjusted trial balance.

f) Prepare an income statement, owner's equity statement, and a balance sheet as of July 31.

(a) and (d)

GENERAL JOURNAL   *Page 5*

Date	Description	PR	Debit	Credit

(b) and (d)

General Ledger

Account No. 11
Cash

Date		Explanation	PR	Debit	Credit	Balance

Account No. 12
Accounts Receivable

Date		Explanation	PR	Debit	Credit	Balance

Account No. 13
Prepaid Rent

Date		Explanation	PR	Debit	Credit	Balance

Account No. 14
Office Supplies

Date		Explanation	PR	Debit	Credit	Balance

Account No. 15
Equipment

Date		Explanation	PR	Debit	Credit	Balance

Account No. 16
Furniture

Date		Explanation	PR	Debit	Credit	Balance

Account No. 21
Accounts Payable

Date		Explanation	PR	Debit	Credit	Balance

Account No. 22
Unearned Design Fees

Date		Explanation	PR	Debit	Credit	Balance

Account No. 31
Brown, Capital

Date		Explanation	PR	Debit	Credit	Balance

Account No. 41
Design Income

Date		Explanation	PR	Debit	Credit	Balance

Account No. 51
Advertising Expense

Date		Explanation	PR	Debit	Credit	Balance

Account No. 52
Office Supplies Expense

Date		Explanation	PR	Debit	Credit	Balance

Account No. 53
Telephone Expense

Date		Explanation	PR	Debit	Credit	Balance

Account No. 54
Rent Expense

Date		Explanation	PR	Debit	Credit	Balance

c) _____

_____

_____

e) _____

_____

f) _____

THINK IT OVER

1. Consider your own personal financial position. Prepare a list of all the assets you own. Place an estimated (or known) value on each. Do you owe any debts? What is your net worth or capital? Prepare your own balance sheet, complete with heading.

    Do the same for your family as a whole. Ask other members of the family for estimated values to place on all assets owned and all debts owed, if you are not certain of the amounts.

2. A balance sheet has been compared to a photograph. An income statement has been compared to a moving picture. What might be the explanation for such comparisons?

Closing Entries

WORDS TO REMEMBER

- **Closing entry** an entry made at the end of a fiscal period to reduce an account balance to zero; to zero out an income, expense, or drawing account
- **Post-Closing Trial Balance** proof of the equality of ledger account balances, debits equal credits, *after* closing entries are posted

SECTIONS IN THIS CHAPTER

- The Closing Procedure
- Income Summary
- Post-Closing Trial Balance

The Closing Procedure

The final step in the bookkeeping cycle is the closing procedure. At the end of each fiscal period, all revenue and expense accounts and the owner's drawing account are closed. In bookkeeping, to close an account means to make the account's balance equal to zero. This is accomplished with a special type of journal entry called a closing entry. The bookkeeper closes all temporary accounts. These include all revenues, expenses, and drawings. Permanent accounts are those that appear on the balance sheet: assets, liabilities, and capital. Permanent accounts are never closed.

Temporary accounts report financial transactions occurring during a specific period of time. It is necessary to zero out or close these accounts after the financial statements have been prepared. That way, these accounts will be ready to begin accumulating dollar amounts relating to the next fiscal period. For example, if financial statements are prepared monthly (and most of them are), the rent expense account should only hold one month's amount of rent.

Temporary accounts list information for a fiscal period and their balances should not carry over to succeeding fiscal periods. Since these accounts show the changes that take place in owner's equity, their balances should be transferred to the permanent capital account in order to bring that account up to date. After being closed, these accounts can be used again, starting at a zero balance, for recording revenue, expenses, and withdrawals for the next fiscal period.

Income Summary

To close an account, a journal entry must be made which will result in posting on the opposite side of that account an amount equal to its balance. The CLOSING ENTRY procedure will reduce the balance of all revenue, expense, and drawing accounts to zero. There are four closing journal entries, and they must be completed in a specific order as shown below.

Revenue accounts are closed first. Since they have credit balances, they must be debited in order to ZERO OUT their balances. The account credited is INCOME SUMMARY, an account used only for this closing procedure. This account is used to summarize the changes caused by income and expenses each fiscal period, and it will not appear in any other type of journal entry. Income Summary is also a temporary account. It will be closed in the third closing journal entry, after all of the revenues and expenses have been closed.

An example of a journal entry to close a revenue account is shown below:

```
7/31  Design Income                    1,500
          Income Summary                        1,500
       To close the revenue account
```

Note that the date of the closing journal entry is always the last day of the month – just as it was for adjusting entries. In this entry, the revenue account, Design Income, is debited. $1,500 represents the balance in that account. When this entry is posted, it will subtract the entire $1,500 balance from the Design Income account, leaving it with a zero balance as shown below. If the business had more than one revenue account, each of them would be debited as part of a larger compound entry. A compound journal entry has more than two accounts. A journal entry with only two accounts, one debit and one credit, is called a simple entry.

Because the Income Summary account is never used for any other purpose, it will begin the closing process with a zero balance. When the above entry is posted, Income Summary is credited for $1,500, which increases that account. At that point, Income Summary has a credit balance of $1,500.

Account No. 41
Design Income

Date		Explanation	PR	Debit	Credit	Balance
Jul.	31	Balance				1500 00
Jul.	31	Closing	G7	1500 00		–0–

Account No. 35
Income Summary

Date		Explanation	PR	Debit	Credit	Balance
Jul.	31	Closing	G7		1500 00	1500 00

The second closing entry will ZERO OUT expense accounts. Since they have debit balances, they must be credited in order to have zero balances. The account debited is Income Summary. Every company will have more than one expense account, so the second closing entry will always be a compound entry. An example of the entry to close expenses for a company with only three expense accounts follows:

7/31	Income Summary	975	
	Rent Expense		600
	Telephone Expense		125
	Travel Expense		250
	To close expenses		

All journal entries must have the total debits equal to total credits. In the above example, the dollar amounts for the expense accounts can be determined by looking in the general ledger for their account balances. To obtain the correct amount for the debit to Income Summary, simply total the credit amounts (600 + 125 + 250 = 975).

Account No. 35
Income Summary

Date		Explanation	PR	Debit	Credit	Balance
Jul.	31	Closing	G7		1500 00	1500 00
Jul.	31	Closing	G7	975 00		525 00

Account No. 53
Telephone Expense

Date		Explanation	PR	Debit	Credit	Balance
Jul.	31	Balance				125 00
Jul.	31	Closing	G7		125 00	–0–

Account No. 54
Rent Expense

Date		Explanation	PR	Debit	Credit	Balance
Jul.	31	Balance				600 00
Jul.	31	Closing	G7		600 00	–0–

Account No. 55
Travel Expense

Date		Explanation	PR	Debit	Credit	Balance
Jul.	31	Balance				250 00
Jul.	31	Closing	G7		250 00	–0–

The third closing entry will ZERO OUT the balance of the Income Summary account. This amount will always be equal to the *net income* or *net loss* for the fiscal period. Take a moment to examine the balance of the Income Summary account in the previous example. The $525 balance was calculated by subtracting $975 (total expenses) from $1,500 (total revenues). This is the same calculation used on the income statement to determine net income. Therefore, the $525 balance of Income Summary represents the net income of the business. If there is a net income, the Income Summary account has a credit balance; if there is a net loss, the Income Summary account has a debit balance. The third closing entry *increases capital* for the amount of the *net income*, or *decreases capital* for the amount of the *net loss*, whichever has occurred during the fiscal period.

The amount of the *net income* is *debited* to Income Summary to "zero out" that account. Net Income is credited to the Capital account, in effect adding net income to capital. If there was a net loss, the debit and credit would be reversed. The debit would be Capital and the credit would be Income Summary. Recall the second item on the

Owner's Equity Statement. Net income is added to Capital (or a net loss is subtracted from Capital). The Owner's Equity Statement provides the calculation of the ending Capital balance. Journalizing and posting the third closing entry actually changes the balance in the Capital account as reported in the general ledger.

Continuing with the previous example, the closing entry for income summary would be:

7/31	Income Summary	525	
	Capital		525
	To close Income Summary		

This entry reduces the Income Summary account to a zero balance, and it adds the amount of net income to the Capital account. Assume the Capital account had a beginning balance of $12,000.

Account No. 35
Income Summary

Date		Explanation	PR	Debit	Credit	Balance
Jul.	*31*	*Closing*	*G7*		150000	150000
Jul.	*31*	*Closing*	*G7*	97500		52500
Jul.	*31*	*Closing*	*G7*	52500		–0–

Account No. 31
Brown, Capital

Date		Explanation	PR	Debit	Credit	Balance
Jul.	*1*	*Balance*				1200000
Jul.	*31*	*Closing*	*G7*		52500	1252500

The following are the closing entries for the Van Loc Company (see page 66). These entries have been posted to the ledger accounts, which follow below.

GENERAL JOURNAL   Page 4

Date		Account Title	PR	Debit	Credit
		Closing Entries			
Oct.	31	Rent Income	41	200000	
		Income Summary	35		200000
		to close revenue acct.			
	31	Income Summary	35	55000	
		Advertising Expense	51		15000
		Salary Expense	52		40000
		to close expense accts			
	31	Income Summary	35	145000	
		Van Loc, Capital	31		145000
		to close net income			

GENERAL LEDGER

Account No. 31
Brown, Capital

Date		Explanation	PR	Debit	Credit	Balance
Oct.	1	Balance				515000
Oct.	31	Closing	G4		145000	660000

Account No. 35
Income Summary

Date		Explanation	PR	Debit	Credit	Balance
Oct.	31	Closing	G4		200000	200000
Oct.	31	Closing	G4	55000		145000
Oct.	31	Closing	G4	145000		–0–

Account No. 41
Rent Income

Date		Explanation	PR	Debit	Credit	Balance
Oct.	31	Balance				2000 00
Oct.	31	Closing	G4	2000 00		–0–

Account No. 51
Advertising Expense

Date		Explanation	PR	Debit	Credit	Balance
Oct.	31	Balance				150 00
Oct.	31	Closing	G4		150 00	–0–

Account No. 52
Salary Expense

Date		Explanation	PR	Debit	Credit	Balance
Oct.	31	Balance				400 00
Oct.	31	Closing	G4		400 00	–0–

A fourth closing entry is needed if the owner has made withdrawals during the fiscal period. In that case, the Drawing account must also be closed. This account has a debit balance, so it is credited in order to zero it out. The fourth and final closing entry also debits the Capital account. An example follows:

```
Brown, Capital                 750
    Brown, Drawing                      750
    To close Brown, Drawing
```

In the journal entry above, the Brown, Drawing account is closed. The Capital account, however, is decreasing by $750. Recall the third step in the Owner's Equity Statement: subtract any owner withdrawals from the beginning Capital balance. Once again, the Owner's Equity Statement calculates the ending balance of the Capital account. Creating and posting the fourth closing journal entry actually changes the Capital balance in the general ledger.

Carefully examine the expanded example below and follow the entries as they are posted to the ledger. Note the debit to the Capital account in the first entry to close out Income Summary, which shows a net loss. Assume that John Wade's Capital balance on November 30 is $12,750 after the first two closing entries have been posted. His drawing account indicates withdrawals of $1,200. His net loss for the fiscal period is $500. Assume that total revenues were $2,500 and total expenses were $3,000. The following are his third and fourth closing entries, which have been posted to the accounts affected.

20__						
Nov.	30	John Wade, Capital	31	50000		
		Income Summary	35			50000
		to close net loss				
	30	John Wade, Capital	31	120000		
		John Wade, Drawing	32			120000
		to close withdrawals				

GENERAL LEDGER

Account No. 31
Wade, Capital

Date		Explanation	PR	Debit	Credit	Balance
Nov.	30	Balance				1275000
Nov.	30	Closing	G8	50000		1225000
Nov.	30	Closing	G8	120000		1105000

Account No. 32
Wade, Drawing

Date		Explanation	PR	Debit	Credit	Balance
Nov.	30	Balance				120000
Oct.	30	Closing	G8		120000	–0–

Account No. 35
Income Summary

Date		Explanation	PR	Debit	Credit	Balance
Nov.	30	Closing #1	G8		250000	250000
Nov.	30	Closing #2	G8	300000		(500)
Nov.	30	Closing #3	G8		50000	–0–

Post-Closing Trial Balance

To prove the equality of ledger debits and credits after the closing entries have been posted, the bookkeeping/accounting clerk prepares a final trial balance—called a POST-CLOSING TRIAL BALANCE. The total of all debit account balances must equal the total of all credit account balances. The accounts will list the same balances that are reported on the balance sheet. The accounts that are open at this point will have balances that carry over to succeeding fiscal periods. These are the permanent balance sheet accounts—*assets, liabilities,* and *capital.* However, the Capital account will now be updated for any net increases or net decreases that may have occurred during the fiscal period. It will equal the ending Capital balance shown on the Owner's Equity Statement.

Compare the post-closing trial balance for Van Loc Company with the Balance Sheet prepared earlier (see page 71). Notice that the balances of all the accounts on the Van Loc Company Post-Closing Trial Balance are identical to the amounts on the Van Loc Company Balance Sheet from page 71. All of the other company accounts are closed. It is not necessary to include accounts with a zero balance on any trial balance.

Van Loc Company
Post-Closing Trial Balance
October 31, 20__

Cash		2 5 0 0 00	
Equipment		5 0 0 0 00	
Supplies		3 0 0 00	
Accounts Payable			1 2 0 00
Van Loc, Capital			6 6 0 0 00
Totals		7 8 0 0 00	7 8 0 0 00

Below is the post-closing trial balance for Fields and Ross. (If a complete general ledger had been illustrated here, all of these account balances would now be shown, and they would be the source of the information listed.) The only differences between the Van Loc Company Post-Closing Trial Balance and the one shown below are at the bottom of the listing of accounts. Fields and Ross is a partnership, so there are two Capital accounts—one for each partner.

Fields and Ross

Post-Closing Trial Balance

December 31, 20__

Cash	2250 00	
Accounts Receivable	3175 00	
Equipment	15000 00	
Supplies	440 00	
Accounts Payable		2050 00
A. G. Fields, Capital		7351 00
B. W. Ross, Capital		11464 00
Totals	20865 00	20865 00

A complete BOOKKEEPING/ACCOUNTING CYCLE has been illustrated in the work done to date. To complete the cycle, follow these steps carefully:

(1) Journalize transactions

(2) Post to ledger accounts

(3) Prepare a trial balance

(4) Prepare adjusting journal entries and post them to the general ledger.

(5) Prepare an adjusted trial balance.

(6) Make the three financial statements.

(7) Prepare closing entries and post to the ledger accounts.

(8) Make a post-closing trial balance.

It may be helpful to visualize these steps as a continuous circle as illustrated below.

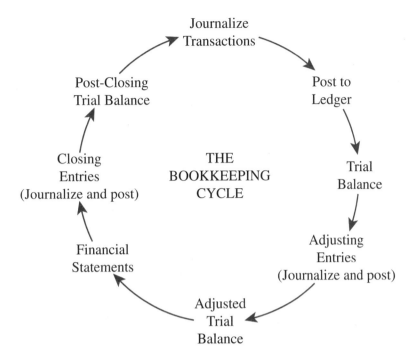

After the entire bookkeeping cycle has been completed and the Post-closing Trial Balance is prepared, the bookkeeper can begin the next fiscal period. All of the revenue, expense, and drawing accounts have zero balances, so they are ready to accept new financial information.

Because the next period's transactions cannot be recorded until the previous cycle is complete, it is very important for the bookkeeper to complete all of the steps in a timely manner. Set a goal of completing the cycle within three business days after the previous month's end.

YOU SHOULD REMEMBER

- The Income Summary account is used in closing entries *to zero out revenue and expense account balances.*

- The *balance of the Income Summary Account* after zeroing out revenue and expense account balances *equals the net income or net loss* for the fiscal period.

- *After all closing entries* are posted, the *Capital account* balance *equals* the amount of owner's equity as indicated on the owner's equity statement and the balance sheet.

- Closing entries are not transactions; they are the bookkeeper's way of *zeroing out income, expense, and drawing account balances* at the end of each fiscal period.

- A post-closing trial balance lists only accounts which have *balances that carry over to the succeeding fiscal period.*

KNOW YOUR VOCABULARY

- Bookkeeping/accounting cycle
- Closing entry
- Income Summary
- Post-closing trial balance
- Zero out

QUESTIONS

1. How are net increases and/or decreases transferred to the owner's capital account?

2. What are the four closing entries in correct order?

3. What does a credit balance in the Income Summary account represent?

4. What closing entry is made when the Income Summary account has a debit balance?

5. What does the first closing entry accomplish?

6. What does the second closing entry accomplish?

7. What is the third closing entry when there has been a net income for the fiscal period? A net loss for the fiscal period?

8. What does the fourth closing entry accomplish?

9. How does the posting of the third closing entry affect the owner's equity?

10. How does the posting of the fourth closing entry affect the owner's equity?

11. Why are balance sheet accounts the only accounts listed on a post-closing trial balance?

12. What does the post-closing trial balance prove?

PROBLEMS

7-1 The following is the adjusted trial balance for Gwen Vreeland, a publisher's consultant and editor. Journalize her four closing entries at the end of the annual fiscal period *after determining the amount of her net income or net loss*. (Note that her withdrawals for the period were $1,800.) Explanations are not needed for these entries.

Vreeland Consulting
Adjusted Trial Balance
December 31, 20___

Account Title		Debit	Credit
Cash		2000 00	
Furniture and Fixtures		5000 00	
Supplies		350 00	
Accounts Payable			1000 00
Gwen Vreeland, Capital			4800 00
Gwen Vreeland, Drawing		1800 00	
Consulting Fees Income			3750 00
Royalty Income			500 00
Advertising Expense		100 00	
Miscellaneous Expense		60 00	
Rent Expense		250 00	
Salary Expense		400 00	
Telephone Expense		90 00	
Totals		10050 00	10050 00

7–1   *GENERAL JOURNAL*   *Page 18*

7-2 Below is a listing of the ledger accounts and their balances for the Allen Insurace Agency.

Cash	$2,800.00
Accounts Receivable	3,895.00
Equipment	4,000.00
Automobile	12,500.00
Supplies	750.00
Accounts Payable	6,000.00
Elliot Allen, Capital	12,920.00
Elliot Allen, Drawing	1,500.00
Commissions Income	8,500.00
Automobile Expense	600.00
Office Expense	175.00
Rent Expense	300.00
Salary Expense	900.00

(1) Complete a trial balance for the month ended November 30.

(2) Calculate the net income.

(3) Journalize the four closing entries.

(1)

Allen Insurance Agency
Adjusted Trial Balance
November 30, 20__

Account Title		Debit	Credit

(3)

7-3 Earl Alpert, an attorney, has asked you to complete the work indicated:

Earl Alpert Esquire

Adjusted Trial Balance

For the Quarter Ended June 30, 20___

Account Title		Debit	Credit
Cash		1605 00	
Accounts Receivable		14580 00	
Office Equipment		3960 00	
Furniture		5250 00	
Supplies		830 75	
Accounts Payable			1875 00
Earl Alpert, Capital			24300 75
Earl Alpert, Drawing		4800 00	
Legal Fees Income			9500 00
Miscellaneous Expense		150 00	
Office Expense		225 00	
Rent Expense		1200 00	
Salary Expense		3000 00	
Travel Expense		75 00	
Totals		35675 75	35675 75

(1) Using the adjusted trial balance provided, complete the following financial statements:

   a) An income statement.
   b) An owner's equity statement. Assume that Alpert's capital was $23,300.75 at the beginning of the fiscal period; he made an additional investment of $1,000 during the fiscal period.
   c) A balance sheet.

(2) Journalize the closing entries.

7-3 (1a)

_____
_____
_____
_____

7-3 (1b)

_____
_____

7-3 (1c)

_____
_____

7-3 (2)

7-4 Pamela Washington is a recent college graduate who has started her own private accounting practice. Her journal and ledger indicate that all transactions have been posted, and she is about to complete the work of the bookkeeping/accounting cycle.

Pamela Washington
Adjusted Trial Balance
December 31, 20__

Account	Debit	Credit
Cash	2,185	
Accounts Receivable	1,250	
Equipment	5,000	
Supplies	580	
Accounts Payable		1,700
Washington, Capital		6,630
Washington, Drawing	800	
Fees Income		1,850
Automobile Expense	90	
Office Expense	100	
Rent Expense	175	
Totals	$10,180	$10,180

(1) Using the trial balance provided, prepare the following for the month of December, 20__

    a) An income statement.
    b) An owner's equity statement.
    c) A balance sheet.

(2) Enter the trial balance amounts in the general ledger as beginning balances.

(3) Journalize and post the closing entries.

(4) Prepare a post-closing trial balance.

(1a)

Pamela Washington

Income Statement

For the Month Ended December 31, 20__

(1b)

Pamela Washington

Owner's Equity Statement

For the Month Ended December 31, 20___

(1c)

Pamela Washington

Balance Sheet

December 31, 20___

(2) and (3)

GENERAL LEDGER

Account No. 11
Cash

Date		Explanation	PR	Debit	Credit	Balance

Account No. 12
Accounts Receivable

Date		Explanation	PR	Debit	Credit	Balance

Account No. 13
Equipment

Date		Explanation	PR	Debit	Credit	Balance

Account No. 14
Supplies

Date		Explanation	PR	Debit	Credit	Balance

Account No. 21
Accounts Payable

Date		Explanation	PR	Debit	Credit	Balance

Account No. 31
Washington, Capital

Date		Explanation	PR	Debit	Credit	Balance

Account No. 32
Washington, Drawing

Date		Explanation	PR	Debit	Credit	Balance

Account No. 35
Income Summary

Date		Explanation	PR	Debit	Credit	Balance

Account No. 41
Fees Income

Date		Explanation	PR	Debit	Credit	Balance

Account No. 51
Automobile Expense

Date	Explanation	PR	Debit	Credit	Balance

Account No. 52
Office Expense

Date	Explanation	PR	Debit	Credit	Balance

Account No. 53
Rent Expense

Date	Explanation	PR	Debit	Credit	Balance

(3)

GENERAL JOURNAL   *Page 7*

Date	Account Title	PR	Debit	Credit

(4)

Pamela Washington

Post-Closing Trial Balance

December 31, 20__

THINK IT OVER

Len Green says he does not make closing entries, nor does he ever prepare a post-closing trial balance. He claims these steps are not needed because he uses only ten to twelve accounts. What difficulties will he encounter two or three fiscal periods from now, if he wishes to prepare financial statements? Do you think the Internal Revenue Service would approve of a tax return based on statements that confuse information from one fiscal period to the next?

Part I Indicate by a check (✔) in the column at the right whether each statement is TRUE or FALSE.

	T	F
Example: All accounts increase by debits.		✓
1. Liabilities and owner's equity increase by credits.		
2. For every transaction, increases equal decreases.		
3. For every transaction, debits equal credits.		
4. A debit to the Cash account results in an increase.		
5. A debit to J. Smith, Capital, results in an increase.		
6. A journal entry is posted to ledger accounts.		
7. The ledger account PR column indicates the journal page number.		
8. A balance sheet describes the financial operations over a period of time.		
9. An income statement is a picture of the financial condition of a business.		
10. The omission of a transaction will cause a trial balance to be out of balance.		
11. A $100 debit posted as a credit will cause Trial Balance columns to differ by $200.		
12. An adjusted Trial Balance aids in the preparation of financial statements.		
13. An owner's equity statement starts with owner's equity at the end of the fiscal period.		
14. Closing entries result in zero balances in revenue and expense accounts.		
15. A net loss for the fiscal period is closed into the capital account by a debit to Income Summary and a credit to the capital account.		
16. Balance sheet accounts normally have balances that carry over to succeeding fiscal periods.		
17. Liabilities – Owner's Equity = Assets		
18. Revenues increase owner's equity.		
19. Revenues + Expenses = Net Income.		
20. Transactions are first recorded in a ledger.		

Part II Match the definition with the term by writing the appropriate letter in the column at the right. Each term is used only once.

Terms	Definitions	Letter

Example: The value in an account → C

	Terms		Definitions		Letter

A. Accounts receivable

B. Asset

C. Balance

D. Closing entry

E. Compound entry

F. Creditor

G. Debit

H. Drawings

I. Income statement

J. Journal

K. Ledger

L. Liabilities

M. Net income

N. Note Payable

O. Owner's equity

P. Post-closing trial balance

Q. Posting

R. Revenue

S. Trial balance

T. Voucher

1. The left side of an account — 1.

2. All accounts arranged by number — 2.

3. Transferring entries from the journal to the ledger — 3.

4. A listing of all accounts that proves debits equal credits — 4.

5. The one to whom a debt is owed — 5.

6. A bank loan — 6.

7. Withdrawal of assets by the owner for personal use — 7.

8. Income earned — 8.

9. Amount by which revenues exceed expenses — 9.

10. A journal entry that zeros out an account balance — 10.

11. Anything of value owned — 11.

12. Net worth or capital — 12.

13. Customers' accounts — 13.

14. A chronological list of transactions, as a diary — 14.

15. A journal entry with three or more accounts — 15.

16. A source document — 16.

Part III *For each of the following transactions, indicate the accounts to be debited and credited. Use the account titles listed at the left.*

Account Titles	Definitions	Account Dr.	Account Cr.
	Example: Received $100 fee from customer.	A	G
A. Cash	1. Paid employee salary, $200.	1.	
B. Supplies	2. Bought $30 worth of supplies for cash.	2.	
C. Accounts Payable	3. Invested $1,000 cash.	3.	
D. J. Owner, Capital	4. Closed the revenue account.	4.	
E. J. Owner, Drawing	5. Bought $500 worth of supplies, paying $100 down and balance on account.	5.	
F. Income Summary	6. Withdrew $150 cash for personal use.	6.	
G. Commissions Income	7. Closed the expense accounts.	7.	
H. Auto Expense	8. Closed net income to owner's equity.	8.	
I. Miscellaneous Expense	9. Closed net loss to owner's equity.	9.	
J. Salary Expense	10. Closed the drawing account.	10.	

Part IV *Country-Wide Plumbing is owned by Chet Gorski. Use the adjusted trial balance provided below to prepare the following:*

(1) Complete Chet Gorski's income statement.

(2) Complete an owner's equity statement; assume that Gorski's capital includes a $5,000 investment during the year. His capital Jan. 1 is $9,685.00.

(3) Complete a balance sheet.

(4) Journalize the closing entries.

Country-Wide Plumbing

Adjusted Trial Balance

For the Year Ended December 31, 20__

Account Title	PR	Debit	Credit
Cash		1 497 50	
Accounts Receivable		385 00	
Supplies		242 50	
Truck		14 850 00	
Accounts Payable			970 00
Chet Gorski, Capital			14 685 00
Chet Gorski, Drawing		9 500 00	
Fees Income			18 620 00
Advertising Expense		480 00	
Automobile Expense		2 400 00	
Miscellaneous Expense		120 00	
Rent Expense		3 600 00	
Telephone Expense		1 200 00	
Totals		34 275 00	34 275 00

(1)

(2)

_____
_____
_____

(3)

_____
_____
_____

(4)

GENERAL JOURNAL *Page 7*

Part V

(1) Complete the following check stub and check:

NO _207_ $ _35.50_		No._____
DATE _January 7_ 20 ____		$\frac{1-315}{860}$
TO _Wilson Supply Co._		
FOR _Smoke Alarm_	_____ 20____	
(Equipment)	Pay to the order of _____ $_____	

	DOLLARS	CENTS	
BAL. BRO'T FOR'D	382	47	_____ Dollars
AMT. DEPOSITED	225	00	
TOTAL			BOLTON NATIONAL BANK
AMT. THIS CHECK			of Long Island, NY _____
BAL. CAR'D FOR'D			⑆0860⋯0830⑆ 1248⋯671⑈

(2) Record the journal entry for the above payment to Wilson Supply Company for the purchase of equipment.

JOURNAL

Cash and the Petty Cash Fund

WORDS TO REMEMBER

- **Bank Reconciliation** a "calculation" made to find the correct, available amount of cash on deposit in a *checking account;* adjust the *checkbook balance* and the *cash account*
- **Disbursement** a *payment* of cash
- **Drawee** *the bank* in which a *checking account is kept*
- **Drawer** one who *writes a check and signs it*
- **Endorsement** *the payee's signature* on the back of a check
- **Payee** the *party to whom payment* is made by check
- **Petty Cash** a separate cash fund used for *small disbursements* for which checks might be unnecessary
- **Replenish** to bring the *petty cash fund up* to the *amount* at which it was originally *established*
- **Voucher** *a special form* used to show *how much* and *to whom* petty cash has been paid, as well as *the date* and *the signature* of the party receiving the cash

---

SECTIONS IN THIS CHAPTER

- Opening a Checking Account
- The Petty Cash Fund

Most businesses make payments by checks drawn on local commercial banks. Many individuals now also use checking accounts drawing on funds in savings banks and/or in money funds. A check is a written order directing the DRAWEE (the bank) to make payment to the PAYEE (the party indicated by the words "Pay to the order of") from the account balance of the DRAWER (the party who signs the order or check).

Opening a Checking Account

When a checking account is opened, each person authorized to sign checks completes a signature card. A deposit slip is used to list items to be added to the account, including checks received from others—paychecks, amounts collected from customers, and so on.

ENDORSING CHECKS

Each check deposited must be endorsed, that is, signed on the back by the payee. There are several types of endorsements.

1. An ENDORSEMENT IN BLANK. This is a simple signature of the payee.

> Gordon T. Barnes

2. A SPECIAL (or FULL) ENDORSEMENT. This states to whom a check is to be paid.

> Pay to the order of
> Willma Higgins
> Gordon T. Barnes

3. A RESTRICTIVE ENDORSEMENT. This limits the further purpose or use of the check.

> For deposit only
> Acct. No. 831456
> Gordon T. Barnes

4. A QUALIFIED ENDORSEMENT. The endorser (payee) assumes no legal responsibility for payment, should the drawer have insufficient funds to honor his/her own check.

> Without recourse
> Gordon T. Barnes

The restrictive endorsement should be used on checks to be deposited. The blank endorsement should be used only when presenting a check for *immediate* payment, for example, when cashing one's paycheck.

MAKING DEPOSITS

Assume that Gordon Barnes opens a checking account and completes the following deposit slip.

FOR DEPOSIT TO THE ACCOUNT OF		DOLLARS	CENTS
	BILLS	250	00
NAME *Gordon T. Barnes*	COINS	—	
ADDRESS *125 Main St. Bolton*	CHECKS AS FOLLOWS, PROPERLY ENDORSED	150	00
DATE *Jan. 2* 20___		300	00
		375	00
BOLTON NATIONAL BANK New York, NY			
CHECKS AND OTHER ITEMS ARE RECEIVED FOR DEPOSIT SUBJECT TO THE TERMS AND CONDITIONS OF THE BANKS COLLECTION AGREEMENT	TOTAL DEPOSIT	1,275	00

⑆0860⭜0830⑆ 1243⭜676⭐

His account balance will be $1,275, and that amount will be entered on his check stub record on the balance brought forward (Bal. Bro't For'd) line. As future deposits are made, he will add to find the total; as checks are drawn, he will subtract to find the balance carried forward (Bal. Car'd For'd).

DRAWING CHECKS

Follow these stubs and checks completed by Barnes for each of these cash payment transactions:

January 2, 20___, Paid Ace Realty $550 for month's rent; Check No. 101
      5, 20___, Paid Security National Bank $300 on loan balance; check No. 102

(Be sure stubs are completed first, showing all information; then complete each check, using pen and ink.)

NO _101_	$ _550.00_				No. _101_	
DATE _Jan. 2_ 20 ___						$\frac{1-830}{860}$
TO _Ace Realty_						
FOR _January Rent_			_January 2_ 20 ___			

Pay to the order of _Ace Realty_ $ _550 00_

	DOLLARS	CENTS
BAL. BRO'T FOR'D	1275	00
AMT. DEPOSITED		
TOTAL	1275	00
AMT. THIS CHECK	550	00
BAL. CAR'D FOR'D	725	00

Five hundred fifty & $\frac{00}{100}$ ～～～～～ Dollars

BOLTON NATIONAL BANK
of New York, NY

Gordon T. Barnes

⑆0860⑈0830⑆ 1243⑈671⑆

NO _102_	$ _300.00_				No. _102_	
DATE _Jan. 5_ 20 ___						$\frac{1-830}{860}$
TO _Security National Bank_						
FOR _loan payment_			_January 5_ 20 ___			

Pay to the order of _Security National Bank_ $ _300 00_

	DOLLARS	CENTS
BAL. BRO'T FOR'D	725	00
AMT. DEPOSITED		
TOTAL	725	00
AMT. THIS CHECK	300	00
BAL. CAR'D FOR'D	425	00

Three hundred & $\frac{00}{100}$ ～～～～～ Dollars

BOLTON NATIONAL BANK
of New York, NY

Gordon T. Barnes

⑆0860⑈0830⑆ 1243⑈671⑆

Notice that the balance carried forward from stub No. 101 is brought forward to stub No. 102. In this way, Barnes will always have a running balance in his checking account.

Each check stub will serve as the source document for making a journal entry. The two entries for stubs No. 101 and No. 102 are illustrated as follows.

20__							
Jan	2	Rent Expense			550 00		
		Cash					550 00
		Check No. 101					
		Note Payable			300 00		
		Cash					300 00
		Check No. 102					

THE BANK RECONCILIATION

At the end of the month, or at a set date during each month, the bank sends each depositor a BANK STATEMENT. This is the bank's record of the deposits made, and the checks drawn *and presented for payment*. These checks are CANCELLED— marked paid—and returned to the depositor with the bank statement. If any charges have been made by the bank for handling this account, they are identified as "SC" ("service charge") and deducted from the balance. The depositor makes a similar deduction on the next check stub. Frequently, the depositor's check book balance and the checking account bank statement balance do not agree at the end of each month. There are several reasons for these differences.

TIMING DIFFERENCES

1. A late deposit, called a DEPOSIT IN TRANSIT, is added to the *check book balance* but does not reach the bank in time to be recorded in the bank statement in the same month—*add any late deposits to the bank balance*.

2. Some checks drawn and sent to distant points have not been cashed (cleared). These are called outstanding checks. *Subtract the amount of OUTSTANDING CHECKS from the bank balance.*

OTHER ADJUSTMENTS

1. If the bank made any service charges, they are deducted on the bank statement— *subtract the service charge from the cash balance.*

2. Checks received by the business are deposited in the bank. The transaction is recorded by a debit to the cash account, which increases cash, and a credit to any number of accounts, depending on the nature of the transaction. Many checks are received from customers as payment on their account. These are credited to accounts receivable. If the check issuer does not have sufficient funds in his/her checking account, the check will not be honored by the bank. The deposit will not be credited to the company's account. These checks are called NSF (not sufficient funds) checks. NSF checks are subtracted from the company's cash balance.

At this point, the bookkeeper prepares a BANK RECONCILIATION to determine the correct, available cash and bank balances. This amount must be the same for both balances at any given time.

Gordon T. Barnes
Bank Reconciliation
January 31, 20___

Checkbook Balance	675.00	Bank Balance	895.00
Deduct: Service		Add: Deposit in	
Charge	3.75	Transit	200.00
			1095.00
		Deduct: Outstanding	
		Checks	
		No. 119, 100.00	
		No. 120, 200.00	
		No. 121, 123.75	
			423.75
Adjusted Cash		Adjusted Bank	
Balance	671.25	Balance	671.25

The amount of cash that Barnes has in his checking account, against which he can draw future checks, is $671.25. If he had not prepared this reconciliation, he might have OVERDRAWN his account. One or more of his checks might have been dishonored because of insufficient funds.

ERRORS

Occasionally, the bookkeeper may discover that the bank has made an error. The mistake might be an omission or an error in the amount of a deposit or check payment. The bookkeeper might also discover an error in the recording or posting of a transaction on the company's books. These items must also be included in the bank reconciliation. It is important to carefully determine the type of error that exists so that it is entered correctly on the bank reconciliation. It is helpful to answer the following questions.

1. Who made the error? The answer to this question will determine whether the item appears on the bank balance or checkbook balance side of the reconciliation. Record the error on the appropriate side.

2. What is the amount of the error? Find two dollar amounts – the amount actually recorded and the correct amount. Subtract them: that is the amount of the error.

3. Does the correction need to increase or decrease the reported balance?

After these questions are answered, add or subtract the amount of the error from the appropriate side of the reconciliation.

In addition to the previous adjustments, suppose the bookkeeper discovers that she has made an error. A transaction for purchasing $72 of office supplies, paid in cash, was journalized and posted as $27. This type of error is called a transposition error. Determine the amount of the error (72 – 27 = 45). The amount of the difference in a transposition error is always divisible by 9 (45/9 = 5).

Answers to the three questions above.

1. Who made the error? The company

2. What amount? $45

3. Increase or decrease cash? Decrease

The original transaction should have deducted $72 from the cash account, but only $27 was actually deducted. To correct this, another $45 must be subtracted from cash.

Examine the Bank Reconciliation for Gordon Barnes shown below.

Gordon T. Barnes
Bank Reconciliation
January 31, 20__

Checkbook Balance	$720.00	Bank Balance	$895.00
		Add:	
		Deposit in Transit	200.00
			1,095.00
Deduct:		Deduct:	
Service Charge	3.75	Outstanding Checks:	
Error in recording payment	45.00	No. 119 100.00	
		No. 120 200.00	
		No. 121 123.75	
			423.75
Adjusted cash balance	$671.25	Adjusted bank balance	$671.25

A properly adjusted bank reconciliation must have the adjusted cash balance equal to the adjusted bank balance. However, this equality does not guarantee that the reconciliation is correct. It is possible for the balances to be equal and the reconciliation to contain an error. This situation occurs when an item has been recorded in the exact opposite place from where it belongs. In the example above, suppose that the deposit in transit had been located on the checkbook side, and that it was subtracted. That would reduce the total of both sides by $200. The book and bank balances would both be $471.25, an incorrect amount.

After the bank reconciliation is complete, the next step is to prepare and post journal entries for each adjusting item on the checkbook side. (Items on the bank balance side are the bank's responsibility.) Since the checkbook balance is represented by the cash account, every journal entry will have cash as one component. All addition items are debited to cash and all subtraction items are credited to cash.

In the example above, two journal entries are required: one for the service charge and one for the error. Since they both result in a credit to cash, they can be combined into one compound entry as follows:

1/31	Miscellaneous Expense	3.75	
	Office Supplies	45.00	
	Cash		48.75
	To adjust the cash account		

The Petty Cash Fund

PURPOSE OF THE FUND

All cash received by a business should be deposited promptly in a checking account. Also, withdrawals are usually made by issuing checks signed by an authorized officer of the business. In that way there is a record of all funds coming in (cash debit) and all funds paid out (cash credit). However, there are times when small amounts must be paid out, perhaps for postage stamps, office supplies, or minor travel expenses, for which drawing a check would not be practical.

A special PETTY CASH fund is maintained for these small payments. This fund requires strict control because of the danger of missing cash. The following procedures are recommended to safeguard the petty cash fund:

1. Petty cash should be kept separately from any other cash on hand.

2. One person only should be held responsible for the petty cash fund.

3. A record of each payment from petty cash should be kept, showing the person to whom it was paid, the reason, the date, the amount, and, if possible, the signature of the person to whom it was given.

ESTABLISHING THE FUND

To establish a petty cash fund, a check is drawn *payable to Petty Cash*, a new ledger account, directly following the Cash account. Petty Cash is an asset so it has a debit balance. The amount of the fund should approximate one month's expenditures.

| NO _376_ | $ _40 00_ | | | | | | | | |

	DOLLARS	CENTS
BAL. BRO'T FOR'D	581	36
AMT. DEPOSITED	400	00
TOTAL	981	36
AMT. THIS CHECK	40	00
BAL. CAR'D FOR'D	941	36

NO _376_ $ _40 00_
DATE _August 2_   20 ____
TO _Petty Cash_
FOR _to establish fund_

ACE TRAVEL SERVICE   No. _376_

1–830 / 860

August 2   20____

Pay to the order of _Petty Cash_ $ _40 00_

Forty & 00/100 ～～～～～～～ Dollars

BOLTON NATIONAL BANK
of New York, NY

Hans Petersen

⑈0860⋯08301⑈ 1243⋯671⑈'

The preceding check is endorsed by Hans Peterson and cashed. The amount is turned over to the person in charge of the fund, to be placed in a drawer or cash box, under lock and key. The check stub becomes the source document for the following journal entry.

20__					
Aug.	2	Petty Cash		40 00	
		Cash			40 00
		To Establish Fund, Check No. 376			

MAKING DISBURSEMENTS

Petty cash DISBURSEMENTS are made whenever small amounts must be paid. The person requesting the amount may be required to fill out a numbered PETTY CASH VOUCHER, giving all required information and signing the voucher. The authorized signature is then obtained to make the disbursement from the fund. The voucher is filed or kept in a separate compartment of the fund box. The following is a typical petty cash voucher.

```
┌─────────────────────────────────────────────────────────────────────┐
│ No. _____                                                             │
│                         ACE TRAVEL SERVICE                            │
│                         Petty Cash Voucher                            │
├─────────────────────────────────────────────────────────────────────┤
│                                                                       │
│                         Date _____ 20 ____                     │
│     Pay to _____   ┌──────────────────────┐    │
│     For _____   │ Amount               │    │
│                                           │ $                    │    │
│          _____    └──────────────────────┘    │
│                                                                       │
│       _____         _____               │
│         Payment Received              Authorized                      │
└─────────────────────────────────────────────────────────────────────┘
```

As the amount of petty cash remaining in the fund decreases, the dollar amount of the vouchers increases. At any time, the two taken together will total the *original amount in the fund*. When the petty cash fund balance gets low, it will be REPLENISHED by drawing a check payable to Cash. The amount of this check will be exactly *equal to the total of the vouchers*. The check is cashed, and the money is placed in the petty cash drawer or box. Once again, the available petty cash equals the total amount for which the fund was established originally.

Assume that petty cash vouchers indicate that payments were made over a period of time for many items. These vouchers are sorted out as follows:

Office supplies	$17.50
Delivery expenses	9.60
Miscellaneous expenses	5.95
Total	$33.05

PROVING PETTY CASH

To *prove petty cash* at this point, the remaining cash is counted. Since the fund started with $40, there should be $6.95 remaining in the petty cash fund. This proves correct:

$40.00	(original balance)
−33.05	(disbursements)
$6.95	(cash fund count)

The replenishing check stub and check are shown below:

NO _387_ $ _33 05_	
DATE _August 31_ 20 _____	ACE TRAVEL SERVICE No. _387_

NO _387_ $ _33 05_
DATE _August 31_   20 ____
TO _Cash_
FOR _Replenish fund:_
Off. Supp. $17.50; Del. Exp.
$9.60;Misc Exp. $5.95

	DOLLARS	CENTS
BAL. BRO'T FOR'D	642	79
AMT. DEPOSITED		
TOTAL	642	79
AMT. THIS CHECK	33	05
BAL. CAR'D FOR'D	609	74

ACE TRAVEL SERVICE   No. _387_

1–830
860

_____August 31____ 20_____

Pay to the
order of ____Cash_____ $ _33 05_

Thirty-three & 05/100 ~~~~~~~~~~~~~~~~ Dollars

BOLTON NATIONAL BANK
    of New York, NY   _Hans Petersen_

⑆0860⑈0830⑆ 1243⑈671⑈

REPLENISHING THE FUND

The replenishing entry prepared from the check stub will result in a debit to the various items for which petty cash has been disbursed. In that way *the only debit to the petty cash account is from the entry to establish the fund*; that will remain the account balance, unless the fund amount is permanently changed. A fund with these characteristics is called an imprest fund. The items for which petty cash was spent will be posted to the specific accounts for which petty cash was disbursed.

Aug.	31	Delivery Expense			9 60	
		Miscellaneous Expense			5 95	
		Office Supplies Expense			17 50	
		Cash				33 05
		To Replenish Petty Cash,				
		Check No. 387				

Petty cash should be replenished at least once each month, usually at the end of the month, or the end of a fiscal period, and whenever the fund runs low.

CASH OVER AND SHORT

In the example above, suppose that there is only $5.95 remaining in cash, and there is still $33.05 in vouchers. As demonstrated previously, the petty cash fund should have $6.95 in cash. This means that the fund is $1.00 short. In this case, the replenishing journal entry will have an additional account called Cash Over and Short. Shortages are an expense, so the account would have a debit balance.

Aug.	31	Delivery Expense							9	60								
		Miscellaneous Expense							5	95								
		Office Supplies Expense						1	7	50								
		Cash Over and Short							1	00								
		Cash														3	4	05
		To replenish petty cash																

The check for $34.05 is cashed and the money is added to the remaining $5.95, so that the total in the petty cash fund is always $40.00. If the amount remaining indicates an excess of cash, it is called Cash Over. The account title is still Cash Over and Short, but it is recorded as revenue, a credit, on the journal entry.

YOU SHOULD REMEMBER

- Outstanding checks *reduce* a bank statement balance
- A bank reconciliation is necessary to avoid *overdrawing* one's checking account.
- Only *one person* should be *responsible for a petty cash fund*.
- The *sum of all vouchers* (for which disbursements have been made) *plus cash* in the petty cash fund must *equal the original amount* of the fund.
- The *replenishing* entry debits the *accounts* for which petty cash was disbursed.
- Only one amount appears as a debit in the petty cash account—the amount for which it was established.

KNOW YOUR VOCABULARY

- Bank reconciliation
- Bank statement
- Cancelled
- Deposit in transit
- Disbursements
- Drawee; drawer
- Endorsement in blank
- Full endorsement (special)
- Outstanding Checks
- Overdrawn
- Payee
- Petty cash
- Petty cash voucher
- Qualified endorsement
- Replenish
- Restrictive endorsement

QUESTIONS

1. Why is a check referred to as a "three-party instrument"?

2. How is a signature card used by the bank teller?

3. What entry is recorded for a bank service charge?

4. Why is a bank reconciliation necessary?

5. Why is it recommended procedure to have only one person in charge of the petty cash fund?

6. What is the source document for the *entry* to establish petty cash? To replenish petty cash?

7. What is the journal entry to establish petty cash?

8. What is the journal entry to replenish petty cash?

9. How is petty cash proved?

PROBLEMS

8-1 Complete Aliza Michele's deposit slip for the following items:

23 twenty-dollar bills	18 quarters
48 ten-dollar bills	31 dimes
16 five-dollar bills	14 nickels
29 one-dollar bills	42 pennies
Checks: $148.65 and $79.15	

FOR DEPOSIT TO THE ACCOUNT OF		DOLLARS	CENTS
	BILLS		
NAME _____	COINS		
ADDRESS _____	CHECKS AS FOLLOWS, PROPERLY ENDORSED		
DATE _____ 20 ____			
BOLTON NATIONAL BANK New York, NY			
CHECKS AND OTHER ITEMS ARE RECEIVED FOR DEPOSIT SUBJECT TO THE TERMS AND CONDITIONS OF THE BANKS COLLECTION AGREEMENT	TOTAL DEPOSIT		

⑈0860⋯0830⑈ 1243⋯676⋯

8-2 Jordan Glaser, owner of a home-cleaning service, completed the following check-book transactions.

January 15	Paid for cleaning supplies, $40; check No. 118
19	Paid for taxi service, $15; check No. 119
22	Deposited $75 in bills and checks for $60 and $40
22	Withdrew $50 for personal use; check No. 120

(1) Complete each stub and check, signing each check as Glaser would.

(2) Complete the deposit slip and enter the amount on the deposit line of the last check stub.

NO ———— $ ————			No. ————
DATE ———— 20 ——			1–830 / 860
TO ————		———— 20 ————
FOR ————		
————		Pay to the
————		order of ———— $ ————
	DOLLARS	CENTS	
BAL. BRO'T FOR'D	136	50	———— Dollars
AMT. DEPOSITED			
TOTAL			BOLTON NATIONAL BANK
			of New York, NY ————
AMT. THIS CHECK			
BAL. CAR'D FOR'D			⑆0860⑈0830⑆ 1848⑈671⑈

NO ———— $ ————			No. ————
DATE ———— 20 ——			1–830 / 860
TO ————		———— 20 ————
FOR ————		
————		Pay to the
————		order of ———— $ ————
	DOLLARS	CENTS	
BAL. BRO'T FOR'D			———— Dollars
AMT. DEPOSITED			
TOTAL			BOLTON NATIONAL BANK
			of New York, NY ————
AMT. THIS CHECK			
BAL. CAR'D FOR'D			⑆0860⑈0830⑆ 1848⑈671⑈

NO _____ $ _____			*No.* _____
DATE _____ 20 ____			1–830
TO _____			860
FOR _____			
_____	Pay to the		_____ 20 ____
_____	order of _____		$ _____

	DOLLARS	CENTS
BAL. BRO'T FOR'D		
AMT. DEPOSITED		
TOTAL		
AMT. THIS CHECK		
BAL. CAR'D FOR'D		

_____ Dollars

BOLTON NATIONAL BANK
of New York, NY

_____

⑉0860⁘0830⑉ 1848⁘671⑊

FOR DEPOSIT TO THE ACCOUNT OF

NAME _____

ADDRESS _____

DATE _____ 20 ____

BOLTON NATIONAL BANK
New York, NY

CHECKS AND OTHER ITEMS ARE RECEIVED FOR DEPOSIT SUBJECT TO
THE TERMS AND CONDITIONS OF THE BANKS COLLECTION AGREEMENT

	DOLLARS	CENTS
BILLS		
COINS		
CHECKS AS FOLLOWS, PROPERLY ENDORSED		
TOTAL DEPOSIT		

⑉0860⁘0830⑉ 1848⁘671⁘

8-3 Helen Spiro's last check stub balance was $420.90. Her bank statement balance dated November 30 was $397.40. A $250 deposit was in transit on that date. Outstanding checks were as follows: No. 217, $75.00; No. 219, $105.50; No.220, $50.00. The bank service charge for the month was $4.00. Prepare a bank reconciliation, indicating the correct checkbook balance and available bank balance on November 30.

Checkbook Balance	Bank Balance

8-4 Yoshi Kawahara, a landscape engineer, received his January bank statement on February 2. The balance was $626.66. His last check stub balance was $708.92. On comparing the two, he noted that a deposit of $375 made on January 31 was not included on the statement; also, a service charge of $3.60 was deducted by the bank. Outstanding checks were as follows: No. 641, $92.50; No. 644, $107.25; No. 646, $37.80; and No. 647, $58.79.

(1) Complete a bank reconciliation, indicating Kawahara's correct, adjusted bank balance.

(2) Record the service charge in Kawahara's general journal.

(1)

Bank Reconciliation	
Checkbook Balance	Bank Balance

(2)

8-5 Hilda Marcello, owner of Space Travel Services, has decided to establish a petty cash fund because of frequent, small disbursements.

(1) Draw a check for $35 to establish the fund on April 1.

(2) As the authorized person, complete petty cash vouchers for each of the following disbursements:

April 2	$2.75 to messenger who delivered a package (delivery expense)
9	$8.00 for postage (office expense)
16	$10.00 gasoline for auto (auto expense)
23	$7.50 for printing business cards (miscellaneous expense)
30	$4.00 for postage

(3) Sort these vouchers; prove petty cash (assume $2.75 remains in the petty cash box); complete a check stub and check to replenish the petty cash fund on the last day of the month.

(1)

NO _138_	$		SPACE TRAVEL SERVICES	No._____
DATE _____				1–830
TO _____				860
FOR _____			_____ 20 _____	
_____			Pay to the order of _____ $ _____	

	DOLLARS	CENTS	
BAL. BRO'T FOR'D	1406	92	_____ Dollars
AMT. DEPOSITED			
TOTAL			BOLTON NATIONAL BANK
AMT. THIS CHECK			of New York, NY _____
BAL. CAR'D FOR'D			⑆0860⑈08301⑆ 1243⑈671⑈

(2)

No. _____

SPACE TRAVEL SERVICES

Petty Cash Voucher

Date _____ 20 _____

Pay to _____

For _____

Amount
$ _____

_____

Payment Received   Authorized

No. _____

SPACE TRAVEL SERVICES

Petty Cash Voucher

Date _____ 20 _____

Pay to _____

For _____

_____

Amount
$

_____   _____
Payment Received   Authorized

No. _____

SPACE TRAVEL SERVICES

Petty Cash Voucher

Date _____ 20 _____

Pay to _____

For _____

_____

Amount
$

_____   _____
Payment Received   Authorized

No. _____

SPACE TRAVEL SERVICES

Petty Cash Voucher

Date _____ 20 _____

Pay to _____

For _____

_____

Amount
$

_____   _____
Payment Received   Authorized

```
No. _____            SPACE TRAVEL SERVICES
                         Petty Cash Voucher
```

```
                    Date _____ 20 ____
Pay to _____
For _____      ┌──────────────┐
                                         │ Amount       │
    _____       │ $            │
                                         └──────────────┘

_____      _____
  Payment Received           Authorized
```

(3)

	DOLLARS	CENTS
NO 156 $_____		
DATE _____		
TO _____		
FOR _____		
BAL. BRO'T FOR'D	1091	37
AMT. DEPOSITED	500	00
TOTAL	1591	37
AMT. THIS CHECK		
BAL. CAR'D FOR'D		

SPACE TRAVEL SERVICES

No._____

1–315 / 860

_____ 20_____

Pay to the order of _____ $_____

_____ Dollars

BOLTON NATIONAL BANK
of Long Island, NY

⑆0860⑈08301⑆ 1243⑈671⑈

8-6 Using the information in Problem 8-5 (1) and (3), complete the journal entries to establish the petty cash fund and to replenish it.

GENERAL JOURNAL   *Page 15*

Date	Account Title	PR	Debit	Credit

THINK IT OVER

1. Timothy Hankins used a qualified endorsement in depositing a check that subsequently was dishonored because of insufficient funds. What rights does the bank cashing the check have? Who is liable for payment?

2. Connie's Interior Designs has a $50 petty cash fund. The owner's assistant, Jim Landers, is authorized to draw checks from the regular checking account and is also in charge of the petty cash fund. Last month, disbursements from the fund increased, and the fund had to be replenished several times. What recommendations might be made to the owner regarding the control factor, as well as the amount in the fund?

The Purchases Journal

WORDS TO REMEMBER

- **Control Account** *a general ledger account* that shows the total balance of individual accounts in a subsidiary ledger (such as accounts payable) and the balances in each of the separate *creditor's accounts*
- **Merchandise** goods purchased to be sold to customers
- **Purchases Journal** a special journal to record *only* the *purchases of merchandise on account* (payment to be made at a future date)
- **Subsidiary Ledger** a separate ledger in which a group of related accounts are placed (all creditors, for example)
- **Schedule of Accounts Payable** an end-of-the-month list of *all creditors* and the *amount owed to each*

SECTIONS IN THIS CHAPTER

- Purchasing on Account—Accounts Payable
- Posting Creditors' Accounts

Purchasing on Account—Accounts Payable

A merchandising business buys goods for resale to its customers; these goods are its MERCHANDISE. This transaction creates an asset account called Merchandise Inventory. Like other assets, it has a debit balance and appears on the Balance Sheet. The usual procedure for most businesses is to buy ON ACCOUNT, rather than for cash. The balance is paid sometime in the future, usually within 30 to 60 days. As a result of such purchases, debts, called ACCOUNTS PAYABLE, are owed to creditors.

PURCHASES JOURNAL

When many purchases on account occur, it is preferred practice to record these transactions in a separate, special journal—a PURCHASES JOURNAL. This journal is used exclusively for recording one type of transaction—a *purchase of merchandise on account.*

There are two methods of recording transactions involving merchandise inventory: the periodic method and the perpetual method. This book will use the periodic method. As merchandise is purchased and sold, no entries are made directly to the Merchandise Inventory account. It is adjusted periodically, generally at the end of the month. Instead, all purchases are debited to the Purchases account. (The perpetual method records changes directly to the Merchandise Inventory account).

The Purchases account records the cost of merchandise inventory. Like expenses, cost accounts increase by debits and decrease by credits. An entry to record the purchase of $500 of merchandise inventory on account would look as follows.

20__						
Feb.	2	Purchases		500 00		
		Accounts Payable/B. Winslow	/			500 00
		Purchases Invoice No. 152				

If there are many purchases of merchandise on account during a fiscal period, this entry will be repeated, and each entry posted to the Purchases account as well as the Accounts Payable account. (Purchases will be numbered 51; Accounts Payable will be numbered 21; all expenses will be *renumbered*, starting with 61.)

Posting Creditors' Accounts

To eliminate this repetitive posting to both Purchases and Accounts Payable, a PURCHASES JOURNAL can be used. Creditors' accounts are posted for all entries so that up-to-date balances will be available. These accounts are located in a separate payable ledger—a SUBSIDIARY LEDGER—where they are arranged alphabetically, or by special account number. Examine the following purchases journal entries:

PURCHASES JOURNAL *Page 6*

Date		From Whom Purchased - Account Credited	Invoice No.	PR	Purchases Dr. Accts. Pay. Cr.
20__ Apr.	2	Tri-Royal Sales Company	4834		3096 00
	7	Thomas Gregorius & Sons	045		375 00
	19	Vincent Merock, Inc.	380		400 00
	26	Thomas Gregorius & Sons	061		250 00

Each of these entries originated with a source document, an INVOICE, a statement or bill completed by the seller of merchandise. As can be seen from the following invoice, this form contains a complete description of the transaction. When received, it is checked against the merchandise that was shipped. Then it is recorded in the special purchases journal. Tri-Royal *sold* merchandise to Best-West and prepared the following invoice. Best-West *bought* merchandise from Tri-Royal and received a copy of that invoice, from which the purchases journal entry is made.

TRI-ROYAL SALES COMPANY
2158 Chamber Street
Trenton, NJ 08609

Sold to
Best-West Sewing Machine Co.   Invoice No. *4834*
296 South Street   Date *April 2, 20__*
Newark,NJ 07114   Our Order No. *7985*
                                   Customer's Order No. *924*
Terms *30 days*   Shipped via *Truck*

Quantity	Description	Unit Price		Total Amount	
18	EZ Sewing Machines #A15	145	75	2623	50
75	Hooks #H107	6	30	472	50
				3096	00

SUMMARIZING THE PURCHASES JOURNAL

The purchases journal is posted on a regular basis (daily or weekly depending on the volume of transactions), to creditors' accounts in the subsidiary ledger. At the end of the month, this journal is SUMMARIZED—totaled and ruled, and the total is posted to the accounts named in the column headed "Purchases Dr. and Accounts Payable Cr." These accounts are in the GENERAL LEDGER. In this way, the general ledger maintains debits equal to credits.

Review the purchases journal below, which has now been posted to both subsidiary and general ledger accounts. Note the 3-column arrangement of the creditors' accounts. This is the same format used by the general ledger accounts. They provide for a balance *on the same line* as the entry—thus avoiding any pencil footings. To determine new balances, remember:

1. Debit entries are added to prior debit balances.

2. Credit entries are added to prior credit balances.

3. Debit entries are deducted from prior credit balances.

4. Credit entries are deducted from prior debit balances.

Look at the money column of the Purchases Journal. The heading shows that all of the transactions recorded there require a debit to the Purchases account (51) and a credit to Accounts Payable (21). When creditor accounts are posted in the accounts payable ledger, therefore, they are recorded as credits.

PURCHASES JOURNAL *Page 6*

Date		From Whom Purchased - Account Credited	Invoice No.	PR	Purchases Dr. Accts. Pay. Cr.
20__ Apr.	2	Tri-Royal Sales Company	4834	✓	3096 00
	7	Thomas Gregorius & Sons	045	✓	375 00
	19	Vincent Merock, Inc.	380	✓	400 00
	26	Thomas Gregorius & Sons	061	✓	250 00
	30	Total			4121 00
					(51) (21)

ACCOUNTS PAYABLE LEDGER

Thomas Gregorius & Sons
515 Capital Avenue, Trenton, NJ 07114

Date			PR	Dr.	Cr.	Cr. Bal.
20__ Apr.	7		P6		375 00	375 00
	26		P6		250 00	625 00

Vincent Merock, Inc.
170 Underhill Boulevard, Syosset, NY 11791

Date			PR	Dr.	Cr.	Cr. Bal.
20__ Mar.	4		P5		150 00	150 00
Apr.	19		P6		400 00	550 00

Tri-Royal Sales Company
2158 Chamber Street, Trenton, NJ 08609

Date			PR	Dr.	Cr.	Cr. Bal.
20__ Feb	28		P4		100 00	100 00
Mar.	18		P5		200 00	300 00
Apr.	2		P6		3096 00	3396 00

GENERAL LEDGER

Account No. 21
Accounts Payable

Date		Explanation	PR	Debit	Credit	Balance
Feb.	8		P4		100.00	100.00
Mar.	31		P5		350.00	450.00
Apr.	30		P6		4,121.00	4,571.00

Account No. 51
Purchases

Date		Explanation	PR	Debit	Credit	Balance
Apr.	30		P6	4,121.00		4,121.00

The creditors' postings on page 148 are indicated by the check marks (✓) in the PR column of the Purchases journal because these accounts have no numbers—they are arranged alphabetically. The Purchases journal total of $4,121 was posted to ledger accounts No. 51 and No. 21 (Purchases and Accounts Payable). Notice that the ledger account numbers are written in parentheses below the column total in the journal. This indicates that only the total amount was posted. Recall that the general ledger PR column provides information on the source of the original journal entry. When posting from a general ledger, the PR is written as G (for general) and 6 (the page number). In the ledger above, the PR of P6 represents the Purchases journal, page 6.

In the accounts payable ledger on page 149, note carefully the three-column arrangement of creditors' accounts, some of which have balances carried over from prior months. A credit posting increases an account with a credit balance. This same technique for posting demonstrated above will be used whenever special journals are involved.

The main purpose of all special journals is to save time in posting. If the previous four purchase transactions had been recorded in a general journal, a total of eight postings would be required: a debit to purchases and a credit to accounts payable for each of the transactions. By using the purchases journal, this has been reduced to two postings. The column total, only, was posted once to purchases and once to accounts payable. Assuming that a typical business has numerous transactions in a month, it is clear that the special journal does save time.

SCHEDULE OF ACCOUNTS PAYABLE

At the end of the month, the accuracy of postings can be proved by preparing a SCHEDULE OF ACCOUNTS PAYABLE. This is a listing of creditors' accounts and the balance owed to each creditor. The total of the schedule should be equal to the balance in the CONTROL ACCOUNT—Accounts Payable—which shows the *total* balance of the sum of the individual subsidiary account balances. A creditor with a zero balance may or may not be included in the schedule of accounts payable. If it is, list the name with zeros in the amount column.

Best-West Sewing Machine Company
Schedule of Accounts Payable
April 30, 20__

Thomas Gregorius & Sons		6 2 5 00
Vincent Merock, Inc.		5 5 0 00
Tri-Royal Sales Company		3 3 9 6 00
Total Accounts Payable		4 5 7 1 00

YOU SHOULD REMEMBER

- A purchases journal is a *book of original* entry, used only to record transactions for the *purchase of merchandise on account.*

- The purchases journal *summary entry* posting is a *debit* to *Purchases* and a *credit* to *Accounts Payable.*

- The schedule of accounts payable *total* equals the *balance* of the *Accounts Payable account.*

KNOW YOUR VOCABULARY

- Accounts Payable
- Control account
- General ledger
- Merchandise
- On account
- Purchases journal
- Schedule of accounts payable
- Subsidiary ledger
- Summarize (summary entry)

QUESTIONS

1. How does one distinguish between a service-type business and a merchandising business?

2. What type of transaction is recorded in a purchases journal?

3. How are creditors' accounts arranged in a subsidiary ledger?

4. How is the equality of general ledger debits and credits maintained when a special journal is used?

5. How is the accuracy of the subsidiary ledger proved?

6. What advantage is there in using a three-column ruling in ledger accounts?

PROBLEMS

9-1

(1) Record the following purchases of merchandise on account on purchases journal page 5:

February	3, 20__	Dye & Akins, invoice No. 1705, $300
	10	Edward Kalpakian & Sons, invoice No. G-116, $425
	17	Dye & Akins, invoice No. 1751, $385
	25	Edward Kalpakian & Sons, invoice No. G-151, $500

(2) Post to the subsidiary ledger.

(3) Summarize the purchases journal at the end of the month, and post to the general ledger.

(4) Prepare a schedule of accounts payable for the owner, Ruth Ann Davis.

(1) and (3)

PURCHASES JOURNAL   *Page 5*

(2)   *ACCOUNTS PAYABLE LEDGER*

Dye & Akins

20__					
Jan.	15		P1	45000	45000

Edward Kalpakian & Sons

(3)   *GENERAL LEDGER*

Account No. 21
Accounts Payable

Date		Explanation	PR	Debit	Credit	Balance
Jan.	31		P1		450.00	450.00

Account No. 51
Purchases

Date		Explanation	PR	Debit	Credit	Balance

(4)

_____

_____

_____

9-2

(1) Record the following purchases of merchandise on account:

February 1, 20__   Paul Olins, invoice No. 42, $175
        5   Wilson & Shea, invoice No. 513, $200
        8   Island Supply, invoice No. 72A, $265
        12   Wilson & Shea, invoice No. 543, $400
        15   Glen Mfg., Inc., invoice No. 31, $620
        19   Paul Olins, invoice No. 78, $360
        22   Gregory Sims, invoice No. 318, $250
        26   Island Supply, invoice No. 29B, $300

(2) Post to subsidiary ledger.

(3) Summarize the purchases journal at the end of the month, and post to the general ledger.

(4) Prepare a schedule of accounts payable for the owner, Maria Zagretti.

(1) and (3)

PURCHASES JOURNAL   Page 2

Date	From Whom Purchased Account Credited	Invoice No.	PR	Purchases Dr. Accts. Pay. Cr.

(2)

ACCOUNTS PAYABLE LEDGER
Glen Mfg., Inc.

Island Supply

Paul Olins

Gregory Sims

Wilson & Shea

(3)   *GENERAL LEDGER*

Account No. 21
Accounts Payable

Date	Explanation	PR	Debit	Credit	Balance

Account No. 51
Purchases

Date	Explanation	PR	Debit	Credit	Balance

(4)

_____
_____
_____

THINK IT OVER

By using a purchases journal, Harold Marino estimates that he saves at least one hour of posting time each week. How is this possible?

Cash Disbursements Journal

WORDS TO REMEMBER

- **Cash Disbursements Journal** a special journal to record transactions *only for the payment of cash*
- **Special Columns** account columns included in journals for *particular transactions* that occur often, thus *saving time in posting*

SECTIONS IN THIS CHAPTER

- Journal Entries
- Schedule of Accounts Payable
- Shipping Costs

Journal Entries

A great number of business transactions involve the payment of cash, mostly by check. Such cash disbursements occur when invoices for merchandise purchased on account are paid, as well as payments for equipment, supplies, rent, salaries, and so on.

With each cash disbursement, a credit to Cash must be recorded to decrease the Cash account. For each of these transactions, there also is a debit to the other account(s) involved. A typical *general journal* entry for a cash disbursement follows:

20__ Mar.	2	Accounts Payable / John Reid Co.			540 00	
		Cash				540 00
		Invoice No. 579, Check No. 318				

A general journal entry such as this requires postings to all accounts—Accounts Payable Debit, Cash Credit (in the general ledger), and John Reid Company's account debit (in the subsidiary ledger). It is preferable, therefore, to use a special CASH DISBURSEMENTS JOURNAL, similar to a check register, which will require less frequent and fewer postings, and still keep creditors' accounts up to date. The entry shown above has been recorded in Jose Garcia's special journal, along with other typical cash disbursement transactions.

CASH DISBURSEMENTS JOURNAL   Page 1

Date			Ck. No.	PR	General Dr.	Acct. Pay Dr.	Cash Cr.
20__ Mar.	2	John Reid Company	318			540 00	540 00
	3	Rent Expense	319		300 00		300 00
	9	Supplies	320		75 00		75 00
	15	Salary Expense	321		150 00		150 00
	16	Union National Bank	322			400 00	400 00
	30	Jose Garcia, Drawing	323		500 00		500 00
	31	Los Angeles Distributing Co.	324			495 00	495 00

Note that there is a special column for the control account—Accounts Payable Dr. While postings are required for each account debited, *special column totals are posted only at the end of the month*. This journal is summarized, and the columns that have *identifiable account title headings* are posted as indicated—Accounts Payable Dr. (21) and Cash Cr. (11). The General Dr. column total is not posted because there is no single general ledger account for that total. Furthermore, the individual accounts listed as debited will have been posted.

SUMMARIZING THE JOURNAL

Garcia's journal now appears as shown below, summarized and posted:

CASH DISBURSEMENTS JOURNAL   Page 1

Date			Ck. No.	PR	General Dr.	Acct. Pay Dr.	Cash Cr.
20__							
Mar.	2	John Reid Company	318	✓		540 00	540 00
	3	Rent Expense	319	64	300 00		300 00
	9	Supplies	320	14	75 00		75 00
	15	Salary Expense	321	65	150 00		150 00
	16	Union National Bank	322	✓		400 00	400 00
	30	Jose Garcia, Drawing	323	32	500 00		500 00
	31	Los Angeles Distributing Co.	324	✓		495 00	495 00
		Totals			1025 00	1435 00	2460 00
					(✓)	(21)	(11)

First the columns were footed; debit totals equal credit totals. Then the journal was double ruled. The General Dr. column total is always checkmarked, and the special column totals have been posted to the accounts identified in their headings. The postings to creditors' accounts and to the Cash and Accounts Payable accounts follow (General Dr. column account postings are not illustrated here):

Notice that the PR column of the journal has a check mark in it for each line which has a debit to accounts payable. The check mark indicates that the creditor's account has been posted in the subsidiary ledger. The PR column also has an account number in it for each transaction that debits an account other than accounts payable. For example, on March 3, the transaction debits rent expense. The PR column has 64 in it, the account number for rent expense. This indicates that a posting has been made in the general ledger, debiting rent expense for $300.

In the General ledger on the next page, the PR column for Cash has CR1, indicating the posting has come from the cash receipts journal (described in a future chapter), or CD1 (cash disbursements journal).

GENERAL LEDGER

Account No. 11
Cash

Date		Explanation	PR	Debit	Credit	Balance
Mar.	31		CR1	5,000.00		5,000.00
	31		CD1		2,460.00	2,540.00

Account No. 21
Accounts Payable

Date		Explanation	PR	Debit	Credit	Balance
Mar.	1	Balance				540.00
	31		P1		1,995.00	2,535.00
	31		CD1	1,435.00		1,100.00

ACCOUNTS PAYABLE LEDGER

Los Angeles Distributing Company

5001 Santa Monica Boulevard, Los Angeles, CA 90002

Date			PR	Dr.	Cr.	Balance
20__ Mar.	4		P1		495 00	495 00
	25		P1		1000 00	1495 00
	31		CD1	495 00		1000 00

John Reid Company

72-05 Canyon Boulevard, Pasadena, CA 91100

Date			PR	Dr.	Cr.	Balance
20__ Mar.	1	Balance	✓			540 00
	2		CD1	540 00		——

Union National Bank
452 Ocean Boulevard, San Diego, CA 92101

Date			PR	Dr.	Cr.	Balance
20__ Mar.	5		P1		500 00	500 00
	16		CD1	400 00		100 00

Schedule of Accounts Payable

At the end of the month, Jose Garcia's schedule of accounts payable is taken to prove the accuracy of the subsidiary ledger:

Jose Garcia
Schedule of Accounts Payable
March 31, 20__

Los Angeles Distributing Co.		1000 00
Union National Bank		100 00
Total Accounts Payable		1100 00

The balance of the control account, Accounts Payable, is also $1,100. The two are equal as the subsidiary ledger proves.

Shipping Costs

Purchases of merchandise may involve shipping charges. These costs may be paid by either the buyer or the seller. The terms F.O.B. (free on board) shipping point and F.O.B. destination are used to indicate who is responsible for payment. This item is negotiated between the buyer and seller at the time of purchase. Shipping point and destination refer to the place where ownership of the goods transfers from the seller to the buyer.

Suppose that Los Angeles Distributing Company sells $500 of merchandise to Jose Garcia. Garcia has agreed to pay shipping costs on the transaction. This would appear on the invoice as F.O.B. shipping point. Ownership of the goods transfers from Los

Angeles Distributing to Jose Garcia at the point of shipment. If the goods are transported by truck, for example, Garcia would own them while they are on the truck. If Los Angeles Distributing had been responsible to pay for shipping costs, the terms would be F.O.B. destination.

The cost of merchandise includes any delivery costs and the Freight-In account is used to record these costs. Using the example above, suppose Garcia receives an invoice for $125.00 from J & R Trucking for delivery charges related to the Los Angeles Distributing transaction. Upon payment of the bill, Garcia prepares a journal entry debiting Freight-in and crediting Cash for $125. See the March 4 entry in the cash disbursements journal below.

A cash disbursements journal may be expanded to include four or more columns, depending on the needs of the business. For example, if many *cash purchases* of merchandise occur, a special column—*Purchases Dr.*—can be included. Some businesses find it convenient to include a *Salary Expense Dr.* column as well. If these columns are included, it is necessary to checkmark (✔) the posting reference column; no posting is needed for each cash purchase entry, inasmuch as *the column total will be posted*, along with all other special column totals, *at the end of the month.*

Examine these entries in a five-column cash disbursements journal:

CASH DISBURSEMENTS JOURNAL   Page 4

Date	Account Debited	Ck. No.	PR	General Dr.	Acct. Pay. Dr.	Purchases Dr.	Salary Exp. Dr.	Cash Cr.
20__ Mar. 4	Freight-in	506	S2	125 00				125 00
7		507	✓				250 00	250 00
12		508	✓			725 00		725 00
19	Supplies Company	509			75 00			75 00
26		510	✓			300 00		300 00
31	Totals			125 00	75 00	1025 00	250 00	1475 00
				(✓)	(21)	(51)	(65)	(11)

At the end of the month, the bookkeeping/accounting clerk can easily see which items need to be posted, and which do not. Those that are already checked *will not be posted*; items appearing in the *General Dr.* and *Accounts Payable Dr.* columns *will be posted* to the accounts identified in the account debited column. The *special column totals*—Accounts Payable Dr., Purchases Dr., Salary Expense Dr., and Cash Cr.—will be posted.

SOURCE DOCUMENT FOR CASH DISBURSEMENT

The cash disbursements journal, a multicolumn book of original entry, is used exclusively for entries that result in cash credits, resulting in a decrease in the amount of cash. For each entry, a check stub is identified as the source document in the Check Number (Ck. No.) column.

YOU SHOULD REMEMBER

- Creditors' account balances should be kept up to date by frequent postings (daily or weekly).
- Special journal column *totals* are *posted* on a monthly basis for the accounts identified *in the column heading*.

KNOW YOUR VOCABULARY

- Cash disbursements journal
- Freight-in

QUESTIONS

1. What advantage is there to using special journals for cash disbursements transactions, compared to using the general journal?

2. How are postings from a cash disbursements journal identified in the general ledger?

3. What justifies the use of a special column in a cash disbursements journal?

4. How are postings to ledger accounts indicated in the cash disbursements journal?

5. When does the check mark (✔) indicate not to post?

6. When does the check mark indicate that the item has been posted?

7. How is the accuracy of the subsidiary ledger proved?

PROBLEMS

10-1 Sid Krasnoff uses a four-column cash disbursements journal with a special column for his personal cash withdrawals. Last month, his check stub record indicated the following:

March 1	Paid month's rent, $400; check No. 247
3	Paid utility bill, $76.50; check No. 248
8	Paid Paula Cory on account, $50; check No. 249
10	Withdrew for personal use, $500; check No. 250
17	Paid employee's salary, $300; check No. 251
22	Paid Hilda Piper on account, $90; check No. 252
24	Withdrew for personal use, $500; check No. 253
29	Bought new equipment, $1,250; check No. 254
31	Paid employee's salary, $300; check No. 255

(1) Record each of these transactions, checking any entry that is not to be posted separately.

(2) Summarize the cash disbursements journal, checking any *total that is not to be posted*. Indicate by open parentheses ( ) totals that would be posted.

(1) and (2)   *CASH DISBURSEMENTS JOURNAL*   *Page 3*

Date	Account Debited	Ck. No.	PR	General Dr.	Acct. Pay Dr.	S. Krasnoff Draw. Dr.	Cash Cr.

10-2 Helen Scordas uses a special purchases journal and a three-column cash disbursements journal. Last month, she completed the following transactions:

April 1	Paid month's rent, $450; check No. 502
4	Purchased merchandise on account from Abel & Jenks, $600; invoice No. P-311
8	Withdrew for personal use $400; check No. 503
14	Paid Abel & Jenks on account $800; check No. 504
15	Paid employee's salary, $325; check No. 505
20	Purchased merchandise on account from W. T. Gross, $1,450; invoice No. 5113
22	Bought supplies, $75; check No. 506
28	Withdrew for personal use, $500; check No. 507
30	Paid W. T. Gross on account, $725; check No. 508

(1) Record the entries for each transaction.

(2) Post the general entries from the Cash Disbursements journal.

(3) Summarize each journal, and post the column totals as indicated in the headings of each special column.

(4) Post customer transactions to the accounts payable ledger.

(5) Prove the accuracy of the subsidiary ledger by preparing a schedule of accounts payable.

(1) (3) and (4)   *PURCHASES JOURNAL*   *Page 2*

Date	Account Credited	Invoice No.	PR	Purchases Dr. Acct. Pay. Cr.
20__				

(1) (3) and (4)   *CASH DISBURSEMENTS JOURNAL*   *Page 3*

Date	Acct. Dr.	Ck. No.	PR	General Dr.	Acct. Pay Dr.	Cash Cr.

(2) and (3)

GENERAL LEDGER

Account No. 11
Cash

Date		Explanation	PR	Debit	Credit	Balance
Apr.	1	Balance				4,500

Account No. 14
Supplies

Date		Explanation	PR	Debit	Credit	Balance
Apr.	1	Balance				50

Account No. 21
Accounts Payable

Date		Explanation	PR	Debit	Credit	Balance
Apr.	1	Balance				800

Account No. 32
Scordas, Drawing

Date		Explanation	PR	Debit	Credit	Balance

Account No. 51
Purchases

Date		Explanation	PR	Debit	Credit	Balance

Account No. 64
Rent Expense

Date		Explanation	PR	Debit	Credit	Balance

Account No. 65
Salaries Expense

Date		Explanation	PR	Debit	Credit	Balance

(4) *ACCOUNTS PAYABLE LEDGER*

Abel & Jenks

1200 Mineral Boulevard, Scranton, PA 18501

				Dr.	Cr.	Cr. Bal.
20__ Apr.	1	Balance	✓			80000

W. T. Gross

805 Keystone Road, Wilkes Barre, PA 18700

				Dr.	Cr.	Cr. Bal.

(5) _____

_____

The Sales Journal

WORDS TO REMEMBER

- **Sales Journal** a special journal to record transactions only for *the sale of merchandise on account*
- **Schedule of Accounts Receivable** an end-of-month list of *all customers* and *the amount due from each*

SECTIONS IN THIS CHAPTER
• Sales on Account • Posting and Summarizing the Sales Journal

Sales on Account

For a merchandising business, the sale of merchandise is probably the most frequent of all transactions. In many large businesses, a major part of sales are ON ACCOUNT, that is, credit sales.

A general journal entry to record the sale of merchandise on account follows:

20__							
Apr.	7	Accounts Receivable / Alan Bergstrom	/		175 00		
		Sales					175 00
		Sales Invoice No. 251					

SALES JOURNAL AND ACCOUNTS RECEIVABLE LEDGER

If there were many sales similar to this one during a fiscal period, this entry would be repeated, and each entry would be posted to the Accounts Receivable account as well as to the Sales account. To eliminate the repetitive posting to both Accounts Receivable and Sales, a SALES JOURNAL is used. Customers' accounts are posted for each entry so that up-to-date balances will be available. These accounts are located in another *separate subsidiary ledger*— an ACCOUNTS RECEIVABLE LEDGER— where accounts may be arranged alphabetically or, in some cases, by special account number. Examine the following Sales Journal entries:

SALES JOURNAL   Page 8

Date		To Whom Sold - Account Debited	Invoice No.	PR	Accts. Rec. Dr. Sales Cr.
20__					
Apr.	2	Best-West Sewing Machine Company	4834		3096 00
	9	Elaine K. Brown	4835		175 00
	23	Ralph Mazel & Company	4836		250 00
	30	Elaine K. Brown	4837		200 00

SOURCE DOCUMENTS FOR SALES JOURNAL ENTRIES

Each of these entries originated with a source document, the invoice or sales slip, completed by the salesperson or the billing department of the seller. This invoice is prepared in TRIPLICATE copy; one copy is given to the customer, one copy is used by the shipping department, and one copy is sent to the accounting department for a source document to record the transaction. (Refer to the invoice on page 147: Tri-Royal Sales Company is the seller; Best-West Sewing Machine Company is the buyer, or the customer.)

Posting and Summarizing the Sales Journal

The sales journal is posted on a regular basis to customers' accounts in the subsidiary ledger. At the end of the month, this journal, like all special journals, is summarized, and the total is posted to the accounts named in the columns headed "Accts. Rec. Dr." and "Sales Cr." These accounts are in the general ledger, and by posting this total, debits will continue to equal credits.

Review the sales journal below, which has now been posted to both subsidiary and general ledger accounts:

SALES JOURNAL   *Page 8*

Date		To Whom Sold - Account Debited	Invoice No.	PR	Accts. Rec. Dr. Sales Cr.
20__ Apr.	2	Best-West Sewing Machine Company	4834	✓	3096 00
	9	Elaine K. Brown	4835	✓	175 00
	23	Ralph Mazel & Company	4836	✓	250 00
	30	Elaine K. Brown	4837	✓	200 00
	30	Total			3721 00
					(12) (42)

ACCOUNTS RECEIVABLE LEDGER

Best-West Sewing Machine Company
296 South Street, Newark, NJ 07114

Date			PR	Dr.	Cr.	Dr. Bal.
20__ Apr.	1	Balance	✓			300 00
	2		S8	3096 00		3396 00

Elaine K. Brown
11 Harbor Road, Perth Amboy, NJ 08861

Date			PR	Dr.	Cr.	Dr. Bal.
20__ Apr.	9		S8	175 00		175 00
	30		S8	200 00		375 00

Ralph Mazel & Company
278 Patriots Road, Morristown, NJ 07960

Date			PR	Dr.	Cr.	Dr. Bal.
20__ Apr.	1	Balance	✓			400 00
	23		S8	250 00		650 00

GENERAL LEDGER

Account No. 12
Accounts Receivable

Date		Explanation	PR	Debit	Credit	Balance
Apr.	1	Balance				700
	30		S8	3,721		4,421

Account No. 42
Sales

Date		Explanation	PR	Debit	Credit	Balance
Apr.	30		S8		3,721	3,721

Account No. 41
Sales

Date		Explanation	PR	Debit	Credit	Balance
Apr.	30		S8		3,721	3,721

The customers' postings are indicated by check marks (✔) because these accounts have no numbers—they are arranged alphabetically. The journal total was posted to accounts No. 13 and No. 41 (Accounts Receivable and Sales). Note, also, that the post reference for the sales journal is S8: sales journal, page 8.

The three-column subsidiary ledger arrangement is used for customers' accounts. A debit increases the customer's account balance; a credit decreases the customer's account balance.

SCHEDULE OF ACCOUNTS RECEIVABLE

At the end of the month, the accuracy of postings can be proved by preparing a SCHEDULE OF ACCOUNTS RECEIVABLE. This is a listing of customers' accounts and the balance due from each. The total of the schedule should be equal to the balance of the controlling account—Accounts Receivable—which shows in *total* balance the sum of the individual subsidiary account balances.

Tri-Royal Sales Company

Schedule of Accounts Receivable

April 30, 20__

Best-West Sewing Machine Company	3396 00
Elaine K. Brown	375 00
Ralph Mazel & Company	650 00
Total Accounts Receivable	4421 00

YOU SHOULD REMEMBER

- A sales journal is a book of *original* entry used only to record transactions for the *sale of merchandise on account.*

- The sales journal *summary entry* posting is a *debit* to Accounts Receivable and a *credit* to Sales.

- The schedule of Accounts Receivable *total* equals the *balance* of the *Accounts Receivable account.*

KNOW YOUR VOCABULARY

- Accounts Receivable ledger
- On account
- Sales journal
- Schedule of Accounts Receivable
- Triplicate

QUESTIONS

1. What type of transaction is recorded in a sales journal?

2. How are customers' accounts arranged in a subsidiary ledger?

3. How is the equality of general ledger debits and credits maintained when posting a sales journal?

4. How is the accuracy of the subsidiary ledger proved?

5. Why might arranging customers' accounts alphabetically be easier for a small business to manage than numbering them?

6. Why are sales invoice numbers listed in consecutive order in a sales journal?

PROBLEMS

11-1

(1) Record Mears's Department Store's sales of merchandise on account in the Sales Journal below, starting with invoice No. 215:

March 2, 20__	Mrs. Edward Ardyce, $175
9	Mr. Herman Gold, $96.50
16	Ms. Eliza Fisher, $107.30
23	Mrs. Edward Ardyce, $62.45
30	Ms. Eliza Fisher, $29.50

(2) Post to subsidiary ledger.

(3) Summarize the sales journal at the end of the month, and post to the general
ledger.

(4) Prepare a schedule of accounts receivable.

(1) and (3)   *SALES JOURNAL*   *Page 31*

Date	To Whom Sold - Account Debited	Invoice No.	PR	Accts. Rec. Dr. Sales Cr.

(2)

ACCOUNTS RECEIVABLE LEDGER

Mrs. Edward Ardyce

305 Riverview Terrace, Cincinnati, OH 45204

Date		PR	Dr.	Cr.	Dr. Bal.

Ms. Eliza Fisher

851 Clarkfield Street, Cincinnati, OH 45201

Date		PR	Dr.	Cr.	Dr. Bal.

Mr. Herman Gold

79 Willowbrook Drive, Cincinnati, OH 45202

Date			PR	Dr.	Cr.	Dr. Bal.
20 __ Mar.	1	Balance	✓			258 60

(3)

GENERAL LEDGER

Accounts Receivable   *No. 12*

Date		Explanation	PR	Dr.	Cr.	Balance
20__						
Mar.	1	Balance				2 5 8 60

Sales   *No. 42*

Date	Explanation	PR	Dr.	Cr.	Balance

(4)

Mears Department Store

Schedule of Accounts Receivable

March 31, 20__

11-2

(1) Record the following sales of merchandise on account for Winslow's Emporium in the Sales Journal below, starting with invoice No. 328:

April 2, 20__	Mrs. Fay Wilamowski, $47.50
6	Ms. Shirley Callahan, $36.95
9	Mr. William Witt, $49.25
13	Ms. Shirley Callahan, $107.65

16	Mrs. Marjorie Intrator, $76.80
20	Mrs. Fay Wilamowski, $52.90
23	Mr. William Witt, $59.20
27	Mrs. Marjorie Intrator, $67.75
30	Ms. Shirley Callahan, $87.00

(2) Post to the subsidiary ledger.

(3) Summarize the sales journal at the end of the month, and post to the general ledger.

(4) Prepare a schedule of accounts receivable.

(1) and (3)

SALES JOURNAL   *Page 8*

Date	To Whom Sold - Account Debited	Invoice No.	PR	Accts. Rec. Dr. Sales Cr.

(2)

ACCOUNTS RECEIVABLE LEDGER

Ms. Shirley Callahan

186 Mineola Boulevard, Mineola, NY 11501

Date					PR	Dr.	Cr.	Balance
20__ Apr.	1	Balance			✓			45 00

Mrs. Marjorie Intrator

91 Bryn Mawr, New Hyde Park, NY 11501

Mrs. Fay Wilamowski

451 Cornell Drive, Hicksville, NY 11803

20__ Apr.	1	Balance			✓			65 30

Mr. William Witt

264 Emory Road, Mineola, NY 11501

20__ Apr.	1	Balance			✓			95 00

(3)

GENERAL LEDGER

Account No. 12
Accounts Receivable

Date		Explanation	PR	Debit	Credit	Balance
Apr.	1	Balance				205.30

Account No. 42
Sales

Date	Explanation	PR	Debit	Credit	Balance

(4)

Winslow's Emporium
Schedule of Accounts Receivable
April 30, 20__

THINK IT OVER

Marshall & Kahn, a neighborhood specialty shop, is considering a change from a one-journal (general journal) bookkeeping/accounting system to using several special journals. What recommendations might be made to help in reaching a decision?

Cash Receipts Journal

WORDS TO REMEMBER

- **Cash Receipts Journal** a special journal to record transactions *only* for the *receipt of cash*
- **Detail Audit Tape** a cumulative listing of all cash register transactions

SECTIONS IN THIS CHAPTER

- Purpose of Cash Receipts Journal
- Schedule of Accounts Receivable

Purpose of Cash Receipts Journal

Receiving cash from customers is another frequent transaction. Cash is received when a cash sale is made, or when it is received from a customer ON ACCOUNT for an outstanding balance due on a charge sale. Cash is also received when borrowed, whether from a bank or an individual or from a cash investment.

In each of the above transactions, the result is an increase in the asset, cash. Therefore, an entry must be made in which cash is debited. The corresponding credit indicates the source of the cash received. A typical *general journal* entry for a cash receipt follows:

20__					
Apr.	17	Cash		75 00	
		Accounts Rec. / Alan Bergstrom	/		75 00
		Payment on Account			

General journal entries such as these require postings to all accounts—Cash Debit, Accounts Receivable Credit (in the general ledger), and Alan Bergstrom's account credit (in the subsidiary ledger). It is advisable, therefore, to use a special CASH RECEIPTS JOURNAL, which will involve less frequent and fewer postings and still keep customers' accounts up to date.

The same entry as shown above has been recorded in Betty Chan's cash receipts journal, along with other typical cash receipts transactions:

CASH RECEIPTS JOURNAL　　　　　　　　　　　　　　　　*Page 3*

Date		Account Credited	PR	General Cr.	Acct. Rec. Cr.	Cash Dr.
20__						
Apr.	2	Gordon Robbins			50 00	50 00
	7	Betty Chan, Capital		2500 00		2500 00
	17	Alan Bergstrom			75 00	75 00
	19	Note payable		100 00		100 00
	25	Mabel Johnson			100 00	100 00
	30	Equipment		300 00		300 00

POSTING TO ACCOUNTS

Note that there is a special column for the control account—Accounts Receivable Cr. Postings are needed for all accounts credited, and are listed in the General Cr. and Accounts Receivable Cr. columns. Column totals, however, are *posted only at the end of the month*, when the journal is summarized. The columns that have identifiable account title headings are posted as indicated—Accounts Receivable Cr. (12) and Cash Dr. (11). The General Cr. Column total is not posted and is checked (✔) because there is no *single* general ledger account for that total. Furthermore, the individual customer accounts listed as credited will have been posted.

SUMMARIZING THE CASH RECEIPTS JOURNAL

Betty Chan's journal now follows, posted and summarized:

CASH RECEIPTS JOURNAL   *Page 3*

Date	Account Credited	PR	General Cr.	Acct. Rec. Cr.	Cash Dr.
20__					
Apr. 2	Gordon Robbins	✓		50 00	50 00
7	Betty Chan, Capital	31	2500 00		2500 00
17	Alan Bergstrom	✓		75 00	75 00
19	Note Payable	22	100 00		100 00
25	Mabel Johnson	✓		100 00	100 00
30	Equipment	16	300 00		300 00
30	Totals		3800 00	225 00	4025 00
			(✔)	(12)	(11)

First, the columns were pencil footed; debit totals equal credit totals. Then, the journal was double ruled. The General Cr. column is always checkmarked, and the special column totals have been posted to the accounts identified in their headings. The postings to customers' accounts and the Cash and Accounts Receivable accounts follow (General Cr. Column account postings are not illustrated here):

GENERAL LEDGER

Account No. 11
Cash

Date	Explanation	PR	Debit	Credit	Balance
Apr. 1	Balance				780.00
30		CR3	4,025.00		4,805.00
30		CD4		3,000.00	1,805.00

Account No. 12
Accounts Receivable

Date		Explanation	PR	Debit	Credit	Balance
Apr.	1	Balance				300.00
	30		S5	1,200.00		1,500.00
	30		CR3		225.00	1,275.00

ACCOUNTS RECEIVABLE LEDGER

Alan Bergstrom

142 Overlook Drive, Minneapolis, MN 55402

Date			PR	Dr.	Cr.	Dr. Bal.
20__						
Apr.	7		S5	175 00		175 00
	17		CR3		75 00	100 00
	24		S5	500 00		600 00

Mabel Johnson

7103 River Road, St. Paul, MN 55101

20__						
Apr.	1	Balance	✓			100 00
	15		S5	220 00		320 00
	25		CR3		100 00	220 00

Gordon Robbins

3216 Twin Oaks Avenue, Minneapolis, MN 55407

20__									
Apr.	1	Balance	✓						200 00
	2		CR3				50 00		150 00
	22		S5		305 00				455 00

Schedule of Accounts Receivable

At the end of the month, Betty Chan's schedule of accounts receivable is prepared to prove the accuracy of the subsidiary ledger:

Betty Chan

Schedule of Accounts Receivable

April 30, 20__

Alan Bergstrom		600 00
Mabel Johnson		220 00
Gordon Robbins		455 00
Total Accounts Receivable		1275 00

The balance of the control account, Accounts Receivable, is also $1,275. Since the balance in the control account equals the total of the subsidiary ledger, the accounts receivable ledger has been "proved."

EXPANDING THE JOURNAL

Any cash receipts journal may be expanded to include four or more columns, depending on the needs of the business. For example, if many *cash sales* of merchandise occur, a special column—Sales Cr.—can be included. If this column is used, it is necessary to checkmark (✔) the posting reference column; *no posting is needed for each cash sales entry*, inasmuch as the column total will be posted, along with all other *special column totals, at the end of the month*. Examine these entries in a four-column cash receipts journal:

CASH RECEIPTS JOURNAL   Page 5

Date		Account Credited	PR	General Cr.	Accts. Rec. Cr.	Sales Cr.	Cash Dr.
20__ May	3	H. L. Wicker			100 00		100 00
	7		✓			500 00	500 00
	10	Mrs. D. Ginsburg			95 00		95 00
	14		✓			625 00	625 00
	17	Lawrence Evans, Cap.		4000 00			4000 00
	24		✓			595 00	595 00
	31		✓			850 00	850 00
	31	Totals		4000 00	195 00	2570 00	6765 00
				(✓)	( )	( )	( )

The bookkeeping/accounting clerk can easily see which items need to be posted, and which do not. Those that are checked *will not be posted*; items appearing in the *General Cr. and Accounts Receivable Cr. columns will be posted* periodically to the accounts identified in the Account Credited column. The *special column totals*—Accounts Receivable Cr., Sales Cr., and Cash Dr.—*will be posted* at the end of the month.

SOURCE DOCUMENTS FOR CASH RECEIPTS

The cash receipts journal is a book or original entry, used exclusively for entries that result in cash debits—to increase the amount of cash. As with all entries, a source document is prepared for each cash receipt transaction; this may be a cash sales slip or a cash register DETAIL AUDIT TAPE, which accumulates a total of the cash register activity for each salesperson.

YOU SHOULD REMEMBER

- Customers' account balances should be kept up to date by frequent (daily, weekly, or monthly) posting.
- Source documents are *business forms* that serve as *evidence of every transaction*, such as invoices and detail audit tapes.

KNOW YOUR VOCABULARY

- Cash receipts journal
- Detail audit tape

QUESTIONS

1. What type of transaction is exclusively entered in a cash receipts journal?

2. What justifies the use of a special column in a cash receipts journal?

3. How are postings to ledger accounts from the cash receipts journal indicated?

4. When does a check mark indicate a posting reference?

5. When does a check mark indicate that an item is not to be posted?

6. How is the accuracy of the accounts receivable ledger proved?

PROBLEMS

12-1 Raul Garcia, owner of the Rose of Texas Specialty Gift Shop, uses a four-column cash receipts journal. Subtotals are indicated for the first 3 weeks' entries.

(1) Continue by recording the following entries for the cash receipts transactions for the remainder of the month:

April 23	Garcia invested an additional $2,000 cash in his business
24	Borrows $2,500 from Lone Star Bank; received a check for that amount
25	Received $85 from J. R. Dallas on account
26	Received $60 from Margo Chase on account
27	Sold old office typewriter (equipment) for $95 cash
28	Received $75 from Frances Lima on account
29	Cash sales for the week amounted to $1,765

(2) Summarize the journal at the end of the month. Checkmark all items *not to be* posted separately.

(3) Post the summary entries only.

(1) and (2)

CASH RECEIPTS JOURNAL   Page 6

Date	Accts. Cr.	PR	General Cr.	Accts. Rec. Cr.	Sales Cr.	Cash Dr.
20__ Apr. 23			75000	143500	597600	816100

GENERAL LEDGER

Account No. 11
Cash

Date	Explanation	PR	Debit	Credit	Balance
Apr. 1	Balance				1,935.00

Account No. 12
Accounts Receivable

Date	Explanation	PR	Debit	Credit	Balance
Apr. 1	Balance				1,729.50

Account No. 42
Sales

Date		Explanation	PR	Debit	Credit	Balance

12-2 Pat Norrell is a wholesaler who sells beauty shop supplies to barber shops and beauty salons. She uses a sales journal to record all sales of merchandise *on account*. She uses a four-column cash receipts journal with a sales credit column for sales made to customers to whom she sells merchandise for cash.

(1) Enter the following sales and cash receipt transactions for the month, in the Sales and Cash Receipts Journals below, starting with invoice No. 7156:

May 1	Sold merchandise on account:
	Willow's Beauty Shoppe, $465
	Lee's Unisex, $395
7	Cash sales for a week, $252.50
10	Received $200 from Goddess of Love
12	Sold merchandise on account:
	Goddess of Love, $268.50
	Jayne's Curls & Waves, $175
14	Cash sales for a week, $307.25
15	Invested an additional $3,000 cash
17	Sold merchandise on account:
	Willow's Beauty Shoppe, $192
19	Received $395 from Lee's Unisex
21	Cash sales for week, $296.80
25	Received $265 from Willow's Beauty Shoppe on account
28	Cash sales for week, $319.90
29	Sold merchandise on account:
	Jayne's Curls & Waves, $225
	Lee's Unisex, $315.20
31	Cash sales for 3 days, $191.40

(2) Summarize the journals. Post to the ledger, posting first the sales journal, then the cash receipts journal.

(3) Post (in chronological order by date) to the accounts receivable subsidiary ledger.

(4) Prepare a schedule of accounts receivable.

(1) and (2)

SALES JOURNAL   Page 9

Date	To Whom Sold - Account Debited	Invoice No.	PR	Accts. Rec. Dr. Sales Cr.

(1) and (2)

CASH RECEIPTS JOURNAL

Date	Account Credited	PR	General Cr.	Accts. Rec. Cr.	Sales Cr.	Cash Dr.

(2)   *GENERAL LEDGER*

Account No. 11
Cash

Date		Explanation	PR	Debit	Credit	Balance
May	*1*	*Balance*				*1,078.50*

Account No. 12
Accounts Receivable

Date		Explanation	PR	Debit	Credit	Balance
May	*1*	*Balance*				*200.00*

Account No. 31
Capital

Date		Explanation	PR	Debit	Credit	Balance
May	*1*	*Balance*				*25,000.00*

Account No. 42
Sales

Date		Explanation	PR	Debit	Credit	Balance

(3)

ACCOUNTS RECEIVABLE LEDGER

Goddess of Love

110 Chemung Avenue, Binghamton, NY 13901

Date			PR	Dr.	Cr.	Dr. Bal.
20__						
May	1	Balance	✓			200 00

Jayne's Curls & Waves

39 Tompkins Avenue, Cortland, NY 13045

Lee's Unisex

451 College Heights Road, Ithaca, NY 14850

Willow's Beauty Shoppe

58 Twain Boulevard, Elmira, NY 14901

(4)

Discounts and Returns

WORDS TO REMEMBER

- **Correcting Entry** a Journal entry to correct an error (usually a posting error)
- **Debit or Credit Memorandum** a business form used to record a *reduction in the amount owed (or due)* because of the *return and/or allowance* granted *by the seller to the buyer* of goods or services
- **Statement of Account** a bill *sent by the seller* to each charge customer that summarizes that month's transactions and indicates any balance due

SECTIONS IN THIS CHAPTER

- Sales Returns and Allowances
- Sales Discounts
- Statement of Account

Sales Returns and Allowances

There are several reasons why customers return merchandise that was sold to them. It may be damaged, the wrong size, the wrong color, or otherwise unsatisfactory. In some cases, customers may agree to retain possession of the merchandise but receive a reduction in the selling price. This is called an allowance. A new account, Sales Returns and Allowances, is used for these types of transactions. Both returns and allowances reduce the amount of money earned from the original sale. Therefore, the Sales Returns and Allowances account deducts from the Sales account. This is evident on the income statement, where both of these accounts appear in the revenue section (Sales – Sales Returns and Allowances = Net Sales).

Sales is a revenue account while Sales Returns and Allowances is a contra revenue account. Contra means opposite; here, it refers to the normal balance of the account. Sales, like all revenue accounts, is a credit, but Sales Returns and Allowances has a debit balance. A general journal entry for a customer returning $25.75 of merchandise originally purchased on account follows:

20__						
May	23	Sales Returns and Allowances	43		25 75	
		Accts Receivable / J. Falkin	12 ✔			25 75
		Credit Memo No. 135				

This entry increases Sales Returns and Allowances and decreases Accounts Receivable. Think about the specific requirements for the four special journals you learned about previously. This entry does not fit in any of those journals, so it remains in the general journal.

Posting references are given to show how this is handled. Accounts Receivable was posted to account No. 12, and Judith Falkin was posted (✔) to a subsidiary ledger account.

SOURCE DOCUMENTS

The source document for such an entry is a CREDIT MEMORANDUM, a form that is similar in appearance to the original invoice but has the words "Credit Memorandum" printed at the top and is often printed on pink paper. A copy is given to the customer (the buyer) who returns merchandise and/or is being given an allowance (by the seller).

Note the use of the diagonal line in the Posting Reference column for the credit part of this entry. Both accounts are posted—one to a general ledger account, and one to a subsidiary ledger account.

PURCHASE RETURNS AND ALLOWANCES

We have just examined a return transaction from the seller's perspective. However, the buyer, or purchaser, also records the return using the account, Purchase Returns and Allowances. It is also a contra account, reducing the amount of Purchases. (Purchases – Purchase Returns and Allowances = Net Purchases.) Recall that Purchases is a debit; Purchase Returns and Allowances is a credit.

The journal entry on page 196 illustrated the transaction as recorded by the seller. The buyer, J. Falkin, would make a similar entry reducing their Accounts Payable and net purchases as follows:

20__							
May	23	*Accounts Payable – Brown Company*	21		2 5 75		
		Purchase Returns and Allowances	52 ✓				2 5 75

The source document prepared by the buyer is called a debit memorandum, which is often shortened to debit memo.

Sales Discounts

Cash flow is an area of concern for many businesses. When a company makes a sale on account, cash flow is delayed until the customer makes a payment. Small businesses sometimes go bankrupt, not from a lack of sales, but from a shortage of cash. For this reason, they want customers to pay on their account as fast as possible. One method of increasing cash flow is to offer a discount for early payment. Known as a sales discount, the payment terms are shown on the invoice.

Many companies offer a 2% discount from the sales price if payment is made within ten days of the invoice date. The buyer retains the right to pay full price (net) in 30 days. This discount offer appears in an abbreviated form as follows: 2/10, net 30. Another offer might be: 1/10, net 45. The first number represents the amount of the discount. The number after the diagonal line refers to how many days the buyer has to remit payment and get the discount. The section after the comma tells you how many days are available when paying full price. While 2% may not seem like much, remember that it is not 2% per year, but 2% for paying just twenty days earlier.

The following example illustrates the journal entries involved. On January 10, Woods Company sells $100 of merchandise to its customer, J. Levitt. Payment terms are 2/10, net 30. On January 10, Woods Company records the sale at its full amount, not knowing whether J. Levitt will pay early and take the discount.

20__							
Jan.	10	*Accounts Receivable – J. Levitt*			1 00 00		
		Sales					1 00 00

20__						
Jan.	19	Cash		9800		
		Sales Discounts		200		
		Accounts Receivable – J. Levitt				10000

Sales Discounts is a contra account, reducing sales, and it has a debit balance. This account is also part of the revenue section of the income statement. (Sales – Sales Returns and Allowances – Sales Discounts = Net Sales)

PURCHASE DISCOUNTS

In the above example, the buyer also records the transactions as follows:

20__						
Jan.	10	Purchases		10000		
		Accounts Payable – Woods Co.				10000
Jan.	19	Accounts Payable – Woods Co.		10000		
		Purchase Discounts				200
		Cash				9800

Purchase discounts is a contra account, reducing Purchases, and it has a credit balance. (Purchases – Purchases Returns and Allowances – Purchase Discounts = Net Purchases)

CORRECTING ENTRIES

Mistakes do happen and the bookkeeper may discover than an error was made in a previous journal entry. Never erase or change a previously recorded journal entry. To make the correction, determine which accounts are incorrect and create another journal entry to adjust them. For example, suppose that the bookkeeper recorded and posted the following entry:

20__						
July	7	Accounts Receivable – Kyle Thomas		45000		
		Sales				45000

On August 2, the bookkeeper realizes that the sale was actually made to M. Fought.

The correcting entry is:

20__						
Aug.	2	Accounts Receivable – M. Fought		45000		
		Accounts Receivable – Kyle Thomas				45000

Statement of Account

Periodically—at the end of each month, or at set dates during the month—the seller of merchandise sends each charge customer a STATEMENT OF ACCOUNT. This "bill" may be in the form of a detailed list of all transactions. Illustrated below is a statement sent by a seller to one of its charge customers:

BOSTON WHOLESALE SUPPLY COMPANY
1219 Beacon Street
Boston, MA 02105

SOLD TO   May 31, 20__

Mr. James Wolff
351 Tremont Street
Brighton, MA 02135

		CHARGES			
May 4	20__	Sales Slip No. 408	2500		
22	20__	Sales Slip No. 573	4000		
				6500	
		PAYMENTS/RETURNS			
May 28	20__	Check No. 79	2500		
28	20__	Credit Memo No. 91	1500		
				4000	
		Balance Due			2500

The charges are debit postings to this customer's account. The payment/returns are credit postings. The balance due is the same as the last balance in the customer's account. Occasionally *a customer may overpay* an account (the balance due). Should this happen, there would be a *credit balance* in the customer's account, an account that normally has a debit balance. (If a creditor's account is overpaid, there would be a *debit balance* in an account that normally has a credit balance.) In bookkeeping, negative amounts are shown in parentheses ($350). This represents a negative balance of $350.

A *cash refund or allowance* may be given to a *customer*. This is a cash disbursements journal entry in which Sales Returns and Allowances is debited and Cash is credited. If the *buyer* records the cash refund or allowance, a cash receipts journal entry will be made in which Cash is debited and Purchases Returns and Allowances is credited.

THE GENERAL JOURNAL

Although special journals save time in posting, there are still many journal entries which must be recorded in the general journal. These include, but are not limited to: adjusting entries, closing entries, many correcting entries, and purchase and sales returns on account.

YOU SHOULD REMEMBER

- Net Sales = Sales – Sales Returns and Allowances – Sales Discounts
- Net Purchases = Purchases – Purchase Returns and Allowances – Purchase Discounts
- Contra accounts (returns and allowance accounts, and discounts) *reduce* the balance of the account to which they are "related."

KNOW YOUR VOCABULARY

- Contra account
- Correcting entry
- Credit memorandum
- Debit memorandum
- Purchases returns and allowances
- Sales discounts
- Sales returns and allowances
- Statement of account

QUESTIONS

1. Why is a sale recorded at full price even when a sales discount is offered?

2. Why do companies offer sales discounts?

3. What kinds of entries are recorded in a general journal?

4. Henry Jones sold $50 of merchandise to Claire Smith on account. She returned $30 of it for credit. What entry is made for the return in Jones's records? What entry is made in Smith's records?

5. What is the source document for Jones's entry? What is the source document for Smith's entry?

6. What information is reported in a customer's statement of account?

PROBLEMS

13-1

(1) Record the following entries in the appropriate journal for Philip Scheiber, the owner of Scheiber's Music Emporium.

May	2	Allowed Jane McDonald $35 credit on account for damaged merchandise; credit memo No. 18
	5	Sold $150 of merchandise to M. Hill, terms 2/10, net 30
	14	Received $100 allowance on merchandise purchased from Baldwin Piano Company on account; debit memo No. 53
	15	Received payment in full from M. Hill less the discount
	22	Allowed Molly Shapiro $80 credit on account for return of damaged merchandise; credit memo No. 19
	23	Paid Baldwin Piano Company balance due of $3,200, less a 3% purchase discount, Check No. 1001

13-1

(1)   *General Journal*   *Page 7*

Date		Description	PR	Debit	Credit

CASH RECEIPTS JOURNAL   *Page 12*

Date	Acct. Cr.	PR	General Cr.	Accts. Rec. Cr.	Sales Discount Cr.	Cash Dr.

CASH DISBURSEMENTS JOURNAL   *Page 11*

Date	Acct. Dr.	Ck. No.	PR	General Dr.	Accts. Pay. Dr.	Purch. Discount Cr.	Cash Cr.

SALES JOURNAL *Page 14*

Date		Account Debited	PR	Acct. Rec. Dr. Sales Cr.

13-2

(1) Record the following entries in the appropriate journal for Carol Dambroff, owner of Carol's Quality Draperies:

May 3   Returned to Home Decorator's Corp, $160 worth of poor quality merchandise purchased on account last month; debit memo No. AR-51

10   Paid $38 cash refund to customer who returned merchandise; check No. 326

17   Granted a $77 credit on account to Robin Moore, a customer, for merchandise returned; credit memo No. 39

24   Received a $50 cash refund for wrong-size merchandise paid for last month

28   Correct $140 error for purchase on account from C. Wilton Fabric Company, incorrectly recorded as a cash purchase

General Journal

Date	Description	PR	Debit	Credit

CASH RECEIPTS JOURNAL *Page 12*

Date	Acct. Cr.	PR	General Cr.	Accts. Rec. Cr.	Sales Cr.	Cash Dr.

CASH DISBURSEMENTS JOURNAL *Page 11*

Date	Acct. Dr.	Ck. No.	PR	General Dr.	Accts. Pay. Dr.	Purchases Dr.	Cash Cr.

13-3 Below is the ledger account for a customer, Pearl Nathanson. Prepare a statement of account, dated May 20, from Hudson's Department Store.

Ms. Pearl Nathanson

972 Riverside Dr.

St. Louis, MO 63104

20__									
May	1		S3		60 00				60 00
	5		S4		75 00				135 00
	12		G2				35 00		100 00
	15		CR5				20 00		80 00
	18		S5		45 00				125 00

STATEMENT OF ACCOUNT

Hudson's Department Store
100 Gateway Plaza
St. Louis, MO 63101

SOLD TO _____ 20 __

_____

_____

_____

		CHARGES		
		PAYMENTS/RETURNS		

13-4 Comprehensive Five-Journal Problem

Daniel Shaw owns and operates a retail jewelry business. He uses special journals for

(1) sales of merchandise on account,
(2) purchases of merchandise on account,
(3) cash disbursements,
(4) cash receipts, and
(5) all other transactions are recorded in a general journal.

(1) Record the following transactions in the appropriate journals:

May 1, 20—	Paid Winslow Jewelers $465; check No. 392
	Paid rent for month $450; check No. 393
3	Received cash on account from:
	Marc Green, $150
	Gian Polidoro, $95
4	Sold merchandise on account, terms are net 30 days, to:
	Antonio Lorenzo, $300; invoice No. B192
	Edward Grabczak, $250; invoice No. B193
8	Correct $35 error for cash purchases of supplies incorrectly recorded as Equipment
11	Sold merchandise on account to Marc Green, $275; invoice No. B194
13	Withdrew $500 *cash* for personal use; check No. 394
14	Paid clerks' salaries, $300; check No. 395
17	Purchased merchandise on account:
	Schmidt & Brendle, $375
	Winston Jewelers, $1,200
22	Received cash on account from:
	Antonio Lorenzo, $50
	Edward Grabczak, $125
24	Allowed $75 credit on account to Marc Green for damaged merchandise; credit memo No. 35
28	Paid Schmidt & Brendle $375; check No. 396
29	Paid $40 refund to customer for returned merchandise; check No. 397
31	Cash sales to date, $2,740
31	Purchased $200 of equipment on account from Allen Co.

(2) Summarize all journals. Checkmark any items, current entries and totals, that are not to be posted.

PURCHASES JOURNAL *Page 10*

Date		Account Credited	Inv. No.	PR	Purchases Dr. Acct. Pay. Cr.

SALES JOURNAL *Page 14*

Date		Account Debited	Invoice No.	PR	Acct. Rec. Dr. Sales Cr.

CASH RECEIPTS JOURNAL   *Page 19*

Date		PR	General Cr.	Accts. Rec Cr.	Sales Cr.	Cash Dr.

CASH DISBURSEMENTS JOURNAL   *Page 17*

Date		Ck. No.	PR	General Dr.	Accts. Pay. Dr.	Purchases Dr.	Cash Cr.

Date	Description	PR	Debit	Credit

The Month-End Process for a Retailer

WORDS TO REMEMBER

- **Cost of Goods Sold** the cost of purchasing items that are sold
- **Operating Expenses** Expenses, other than Cost of Goods Sold, incurred during the daily operation of the business

SECTIONS IN THIS CHAPTER

- Income Statement
- Closing Entries

In Chapters 6 and 7, you learned about the final steps in the bookkeeping cycle: financial statements and closing entries. A retail business also prepares financial statements and closing entries, but these are impacted somewhat by the additional accounts introduced in Chapters 9–13. With the exception of merchandise inventory, all of the new accounts are temporary accounts, relating to either revenues or expenses.

Income Statement

For this reason, we will examine the income statement for a merchandising company. Recall that the basic format of any income statement is:

Revenues – Expenses = Net Income.

Its purpose is to determine whether the company earned a profit during the fiscal period.

The expanded revenue section now contains the following:

Sales – Sales Discounts – Sales Returns and Allowances = Net Sales

The Sales account represents total sales, while Net Sales is the actual dollar amount the company expects to receive. Net Sales is not an account title, but refers to the subtotal of the revenue section.

The expense portion of the income statement is divided into two parts: Cost of Goods Sold and Operating Expenses. All of the accounts related to the purchase of merchandise are in the cost of goods sold section. Operating Expenses consists of those expense accounts illustrated in the income statement from Chapter 6, i.e., supplies expense, salary expense and so on.

Cost of Goods Sold (CGS) is a calculation to determine the full cost of purchasing those items which have been sold during the current fiscal period. Begin by calculating net purchases:

Purchases – Purchase Discounts – Purchase Returns and Allowances = Net Purchases

Purchase Discounts and Purchase Returns and Allowances are subtracted because they represent money which will not be paid by the buyer. Net Purchases is also a subtitle, not the name of a particular account.

Net Purchases and Freight-in are added together to arrive at Cost of Goods Purchased, the total cost of purchasing the merchandise. Recall that shipping charges (Freight-In) are included in the cost of an item.

Net Purchases + Freight-In = Cost of Goods Purchased

To determine exactly what was sold during the fiscal period, it is necessary to include both the beginning and ending inventory. Beginning inventory is the amount of merchandise on hand at the start of the fiscal period. Cost of Goods Purchased is added to beginning inventory: the result is called Goods Available for Sale.

Beginning Inventory + Cost of Goods Purchased = Goods Available for Sale

This subtotal is the amount of merchandise that could have been sold. However, businesses never sell all of their merchandise by the end of the month. There are always items remaining on the store shelves and in storage, which are available to serve customers at the start of the next month. Therefore, subtract the Ending Inventory from Goods Available for Sale to arrive at the Cost of Goods Sold.

Goods Available for Sale – Ending Inventory = Cost of Goods Sold.

The next calculation assists the business in determining its profit margin on items sold. For example, a retail store sells television sets for $500. These televisions were purchased from the manufacturer at a net cost of $300. The profit margin is $200 per set (500 – 300). On the income statement, this is called Gross Profit, or sometimes, Gross Margin.

Net Sales – Cost of Goods Sold = Gross Profit

Operating Expenses are then subtracted from Gross Profit to determine net income. This section includes all of the business's expenses except for those already reported in the Cost of Goods Sold section. These, generally, are those accounts with the word "expense" in the title.

Gross Profit – Operating Expenses = Net Income

Examine the income statement that follows. It is for a retailer and begins with the customary three-line heading: company name, report title, and date.

Aaron's Sporting Goods				
Income Statement				
For the month ended April 30, 20___				

Revenues:				
Sales		$155000		
Less: Sales Discounts	30000			
Sales Returns and Allowances	12000	42000		
Net Sales				1508000
Cost of Goods Sold:				
Merchandise Inventory, April 1			180000	
Purchases	1000000			
Less: Purchase Discounts	36000			
Purchase Returns and Allowances	20000			
Net Purchases		944000		
Add: Freight-In		50000		
Cost of Goods Purchased			994000	
Goods Available for Sale			1174000	
Less: Merchandise Inventory, April 30			195000	
Cost of Goods Sold				979000
Gross Profit				529000
Operating Expenses:				
Advertising Expense		45000		
Rent Expense		90000		
Salary Expense		82500		
Supplies Expense		12500		
Total Operating Expenses				230000
Net Income				$299000

The number of columns needed for any financial statement is determined by the amount of subtotals. Because these reports are prepared for many users, both inside and outside of the company, it is important for them to be clear and easy to follow. Numbers added together or subtracted from each other should not have any other numbers in between.

The income statement accounted for all of the retail accounts except for Merchandise Inventory. This asset account records the amount of inventory on hand. When additional purchases are made during the month, the Purchases account increases. The Merchandise Inventory account is not increased at that time. Likewise, this account does not decrease when sales occur. Instead, the Merchandise Inventory account is adjusted as part of the Closing Entries previously discussed in Chapter 7.

Closing Entries

Recall that there are four closing entries: close revenues, close expenses, close income summary, and close drawings. Prior to adjustment, Merchandise Inventory will show the amount of beginning inventory. In order to change that amount from beginning to ending inventory, simply alter the first two closing entries, removing the beginning inventory amount by crediting the account. Replace it with the ending inventory by debiting it. The following closing entries zero out all of the temporary accounts for Aaron's Sporting Goods, and adjust its inventory account. The temporary accounts include all of the new accounts relating to purchases and sales, as well as the revenue and expense accounts. In addition to the above, Aaron withdrew $600 for personal use.

1.

Date	Description	PR	Debit	Credit
	Merchandise inventory		1950 00	
	Sales		15500 00	
	Purchase Discounts		360 00	
	Purchase Returns & Allowances		200 00	
	Income Summary			18010 00

To close all temporary accounts having a credit balance and record the ending inventory

2.

Date	Description	PR	Debit	Credit
	Income Summary		15020 00	
	Sales Discounts			300 00
	Sales Returns & Allowances			120 00
	Purchases			10000 00
	Freight-In			500 00
	Advertising Expense			450 00
	Rent Expense			900 00
	Salary Expense			825 00
	Supplies Expense			125 00
	Merchandise Inventory			1800 00

To close all temporary accounts having a debit balance and remove the beginning inventory

3.

Date		Description	PR	Debit	Credit
		Income Summary		2 9 9 0 00	
		Aaron's Capital			2 9 9 0 00

To close Income Summary, adding net income to Capital

4.

Date		Description	PR	Debit	Credit
		Aaron's Capital		6 0 0 00	
		Aaron's Drawing			6 0 0 00

To close Drawing and subtract it from Capital

YOU SHOULD REMEMBER

- Close all temporary accounts and adjust the Merchandise Inventory account.
- A company should have enough gross profit to cover all of its operating expenses and provide a profit.

KNOW YOUR VOCABULARY

- Cost of Goods Purchased
- Cost of Goods Sold
- Goods Available for Sale
- Gross Profit
- Operating Expenses

QUESTIONS

1. What is included in the financial statement heading?

2. What are the three sections of the income statement for a retailer?

3. Why is freight-in added to net purchases?

4. How is the merchandise inventory account adjusted from the beginning to the ending inventory amount?

PROBLEMS

14-1 The general ledger for Jan's Appliance Warehouse shows the following accounts:

Purchases	$200	Sales Discounts	$30
Purchase Discounts	40	Advertising Expense	20
Sales	1,000	Freight-In	15
Sales Returns & Allowances	20	Supplies Expense	10
Merchandise Inventory, July 1	400	Rent Expense	100
Salary Expense	150	Merchandise Inventory, July 31	300
Purchase Returns & Allowances	25	Jan's, Drawings	50

(a) Calculate Net Sales

(b) Calculate Net Purchases

(c) Calculate Cost of Goods Purchased

(d) Calculate Goods Available for Sale

14-2 Using the information from Problem 14-1, prepare an income statement in good form.

14-3 Prepare closing entries for Jan's Appliance Warehouse.

GENERAL JOURNAL

Date	Description	PR	Debit	Credit

Computerized Bookkeeping

WORDS TO REMEMBER

This chapter focuses on bookkeeping software that can save time and eliminate errors. In this chapter you will learn:

- **Bookkeeping Software** programs that can be used to increase the accuracy and speed of a business's bookkeeping
- **Customizing Accounts** ways to customize software templates for the needs of the business
- **Entering Information** manually entering data into bookkeeping software
- **Software Functions** generating ledgers, payroll, tax forms, and much more

Bookkeeping Software

Even the smallest business today probably uses some type of bookkeeping software. These packages are inexpensive and can provide two major benefits: time savings and error reduction. Most accounting software offers a variety of ways to customize financial reporting to suit the needs of many types of businesses.

RESPONSIBILITIES OF THE BOOKKEEPER

Although many of the bookkeeping functions are automated when using software, the bookkeeping cycle and all of the related steps remain intact. It is still necessary for the bookkeeper to be familiar with these procedures to ensure proper recording of all financial transactions. In the event that errors occur when journalizing, it is important to have a thorough understanding of the rules of debits and credits in order to make the necessary corrections. For these reasons, most people begin learning about accounting with a manual approach, as was demonstrated in this book.

After the basics have been mastered, it is easy to transfer your knowledge to a computerized system. Two popular packages for small to medium sized businesses are Peachtree and QuickBooks. Although there are some differences, both of them provide good user support to get businesses up and running in a short time. Setting up your business using software is very similar to a manual setup.

CHART OF ACCOUNTS

The first step is to create the chart of accounts. There will be many different preset charts of accounts to choose from, defined by the type of business. For example, if you choose hair salon, a list of accounts that might be found in a typical hair salon will appear. The bookkeeper can then customize the list by deleting, adding, or changing account titles.

After the chart of accounts is set, enter the beginning balances for all of the permanent accounts. Remember that these are the balance sheet accounts: assets, liabilities, and capital. Choose the reports feature, and display a trial balance to check that debits equal credits. Other information to enter before recording transactions might include customer and vendor data, such as name, address, credit terms, etc. For a service business, enter information on common services provided and their costs. For a merchandiser, enter inventory items, including descriptions, costs, item numbers, etc.

All of this data is entered at the beginning so that future transactions can be entered quickly and efficiently. One of the ways computerized systems save time is by allowing the bookkeeper to select data by clicking on an item, rather than having to write everything in. When recording a sale, the customer list provides all of the relevant information, which will automatically be entered on the invoice.

Another time saver relates to the various mathematical functions required. The software performs any adding, multiplying, etc., which also eliminates many of the errors found in manual bookkeeping systems. If the business sells 10 lawnmowers @ $200 each, the multiplication will occur automatically and the total cost of $2,000 will be entered on the invoice. Special journals and general and subsidiary ledgers all involve a lot of addition and subtraction. This not only provides many opportunities for mistakes to occur, finding and correcting each error is very time intensive. Therefore, the bookkeeper saves time two ways: first, by not having to perform numerous calculations, and later, by not having to correct errors.

Accounting software is very helpful in processing payroll. Federal, state, and local income taxes each have their own rates and reporting requirements. There are also worker's compensation and unemployment taxes to consider. Subscriptions are available that will keep software continuously updated for any changes in tax rates or regulations. Again, the many calculations are automated and reports can be generated for filing the various tax forms.

Posting and Generating Reports

The second step in the bookkeeping cycle, posting, is accomplished with the click of a button in a computerized system. Just click "post" and journal entries are automatically transferred to the general and subsidiary ledgers. Many errors originate from the posting process in a manual system. Numbers are transposed, entries are recorded in the wrong account, and entire transactions can be omitted. These types of problems are much less likely to occur when software is used.

One part of the bookkeeping cycle that still requires significant attention is adjusting entries. These must be generated by the bookkeeper and entered into the general journal, much like the manual approach. However, if the same entry occurs monthly (adjusting prepaid insurance for a set amount each month, for example), a recurring adjustment can be programmed to automatically be recorded.

Reports are generated easily. The reports section will offer a wide variety of financial statements, trial balances, and other reports that can be created just by selecting and clicking on the report name. Lists of open invoices can be sorted by customer for accounts receivable or by vendor for accounts payable. Sales reports assist the owner in managing inventory by focusing attention on fast or slow moving items. The ease of creating these reports will enable the business owner to receive more detailed and helpful feedback to evaluate and assess the business operations.

Accounting software provides even the smallest business with many important advantages. These include:

- Convenience
- Ease of use
- Time savings
- Reasonable cost
- Error reduction
- Improved management information

QUESTIONS

1. Name two popular accounting software packages.

2. What are some advantages of using a computerized system?

3. How is posting accomplished in a computerized system?

4. How can reports help the business owner/manager?

Part I *Indicate by a check (✔) in the column at the right whether each statement is TRUE or FALSE.*

		T	F
Example: Debts owed to creditors are accounts payable.		✓	
1. A purchases journal is used for recording the purchase of all merchandise on account.	1.		
2. Cost accounts increase by debits.	2.		
3. A major advantage of special journals is the elimination of repetitive posting.	3.		
4. A source document for each transaction is identified in the ledger account.	4.		
5. A control account is found in each subsidiary ledger.	5.		
6. A summary entry proves that debits equal credits in each journal.	6.		
7. A check mark posting reference to a cutomer's account indicates that the item has been posted.	7.		
8. General Debit and General Credit column totals are posted to general ledger accounts.	8.		
9. A subsidiary ledger's accuracy is proved by preparing a trial balance.	9.		
10. Invoices usually are prepared in multiple copies.	10.		
11. The use of special journals eliminates the need for control accounts.	11.		
12. A correcting entry usually is recorded in the general journal.	12.		
13. A charge to the wrong customer's account is corrected by debiting that account and crediting the correct one.	13.		
14. A withdrawal of merchandise by the owners is debited to the Sales account.	14		
15. A statement of account is sent to each charge customer to indicate the balance due.	15.		
16. A bank statement will identify outstanding checks.	16.		
17. Each petty cash voucher is the source document for a journal entry.	17.		
18. Partners automatically share net income equally unless a written agreement specifies otherwise.	18.		
19. Gross profit on sales is found by subtracting cost of goods sold from net sales.	19.		
20. A post-closing trial balance includes general ledger accounts with adjusted balances.	20.		

Part II *Match the definition with the term by writing the appropriate* letter *in the column at the right (A term is used only once.)*

Terms	Definitions	Letter

Terms

A. Adjusting entries
B. Balance sheet
C. Cash disbursements journal
D. Cash receipts journal
E. Closing entries
F. Debit
G. Credit
H. General journal
I. Income statement
J. Invoice
K. On account
L. Purchase returns and allowances
M. Subsidiary ledger
N. Summary entry
O. Trial balance

Definitions

Example: A charge purchase of merchandise, rather than a purchase for cash

1. A special grouping of similar accounts
2. A source document that describes a sale of merchandise
3. The totaling of all special journals to prove that debits equal credits
4. A special journal for all cash payments.
5. The journal in which a cash sale is recorded.
6. The normal balance of a customer's account receivable.
7. A contra account
8. Entries made at the end of the fiscal period to bring certain accounts up to date.
9. The financial statement that determines profit or loss.
10. Proves that general ledger debits and credits are equal
11. The journal in which adjusting entries are recorded.

Letter

	K
1.	
2.	
3.	
4.	
5.	
6.	
7.	
8.	
9.	
10.	
11.	

Part III

(1) Record each of the following transactions for Rex Drug Company in the journals provided:

June 1	Paid month's rent, $375; check No. 147
3	Purchased $500 worth of merchandise on account from J. L. Rossini Company
5	Sold merchandise on account to Dr. George Tyler, $165; invoice No. 452
8	The owner, Jordan Glaser, withdrew $50 worth of merchandise for personal use
10	Paid J. L. Rossini Company $500 on account; check No. 148
12	Issued credit memo No. 7 for $15 to Dr. George Tyler for merchandise returned
15	Cash sales to date were $2,950
19	Paid telephone bill, $46; check No. 149
22	Received $150 from Dr. George Tyler for balance due on account
26	Sold $125 worth of merchandise to Sonia Parisian on account; invoice No. 453
29	Purchased $300 worth of merchandise from Fred Pulaski Wholesalers, Inc., on account
30	Cash sales to date were $3,750

(2) Summarize each journal, and checkmark any totals not to be posted.

(1)

GENERAL JOURNAL

Date	Description	PR	Debit	Credit

(1) and (2)

PURCHASES JOURNAL   Page 3

Date	Account Credited	PR	Purchases Dr. Accts. Pay. Cr.

SALES JOURNAL   Page 3

Date	Account Debited	Invoice No.	PR	Accts. Rec. Dr. Sales Cr.

(1) and (2)

CASH RECEIPTS JOURNAL   *Page 4*

Date	Account Credited	PR	General Cr.	Accts. Rec. Cr.	Sales Cr.	Cash Dr.

Page 3

(1) and (2)

CASH DISBURSEMENTS JOURNAL

Date	Account Debited	Ck. No.	PR	General Dr.	Accts. Pay. Dr.	Purchases Dr.	Salary Exp. Dr.	Cash Cr.

Part IV

Using the adjusted trial balance provided below for Annie's Flower Emporium:

(1) Prepare an income statement

(2) Journalize the closing entries

	Annie's Flower Emporium		
	Adjusted Trial Balance		
	For the month ended August 31, 20__		

		Debit	Credit
Cash		3 2 0 0 00	
Accounts Receivable		7 5 0 00	
Merchandise Inventory, August 1		1 6 0 0 00	
Fixtures		2 3 0 0 00	
Prepaid Insurance		4 0 0 00	
Supplies		1 5 0 00	
Accounts Payable			1 3 5 0 00
Annie's Capital			4 6 8 0 00
Annie's Drawings		2 0 0 00	
Sales			1 3 0 0 0 00
Sales Returns and Allowances		1 2 5 00	
Sales Discounts		2 3 0 00	
Purchases		8 0 0 0 00	
Purchases Returns and Allowances			5 5 0 00
Purchase Discounts			1 3 0 00
Advertising Expense		4 0 0 00	
Freight-In		3 0 0 00	
Insurance Expense		2 0 0 00	
Miscellaneous Expense		1 8 0 00	
Rent Expense		6 5 0 00	
Salaries Expense		9 0 0 00	
Supplies Expense		1 2 5 00	
Totals		$ 1 9 7 1 0 00	$ 1 9 7 1 0 00

*Merchandise Inventory on August 31 is $1,500.

(1)

(2)

GENERAL JOURNAL

Date		Description	PR	Debit	Credit

Answer Key

Chapter 1

QUESTIONS

1–1

	Classification	Side
1.	Asset	Left
2.	Liability	Right
3.	Owner's equity	Right
4.	Asset	Left
5.	Liability	Right
6.	Asset	Left
7.	Asset	Left
8.	Liability	Right
9.	Asset	Left
10.	Asset	Left

1-2 Winslow's liabilities total $5,000 compared to Calhoun's liabilities of $7,500. Winslow also has $7,500 more in assets. She is in a stronger financial situation. It would be helpful to know how much cash each individual has.

1-3 Loan for $14,000 ($20,000 − $6,000)
Fundamental equation:
Assets increase $14,000   Liabilities increase $14,000, Owner's Equity, no change

PROBLEMS

1–1

1.	$ 11,500.00
2.	3,700.00
3.	17,500.00
4.	16,087.10
5.	8,569.07
6.	106,930.96
7.	210,818.34
8.	40,314.48
9.	571,657.75
10.	1,116,743.28

1-2

	A	= L	+ OE
1.	Decrease	Decrease	
2.	None		
3.	Increase	Increase	
4.	None		
5.	None		
6.	Increase		Increase
7.	Increase	Increase	
8.	Decrease		Decrease

1-3

	A	= L	+ OE
1.	−$ 2,000 + 2,000 $29,250	$ 4,250	$25,000
2.	+ 7,500 $36,750	+ 7,500 $11,750	$25,000
3.	−$ 450 + 450 $36,750	$11,750	$25,000
4.	−$12,000 + 12,000 $36,750	$11,750	$25,000
5.	− 1,500 $35,250	− 1,500 $10,250	$25,000

Chapter 2

QUESTIONS

2-1. (a) shorten pants, waist adjustments
(b) hair cut, manicure
(c) plans for new or rebuilding homes
(d) drawing up legal documents, defending a client
(e) tooth extraction, cleaning teeth
(f) preparing financial statements, tax returns

2-2. (a) heat, light, sewing supplies
(b) salaries, utilities
(c) office rent, supplies
(d) salaries, legal forms
(e) salaries, supplies
(f) supplies, auto expense

PROBLEMS

2-1

	Assets	+		Expenses	+	Drawings	=	Liabilities	+ Revenues	+ Capital
	Cash + Taxis	+ Gas Exp.	+ Rep. Exp.	+ Sal. Exp.	+ Drawings	=	N/P + A/P	+ Fare Inc.	+ Capital

Bal.	712 + 28,000	+ 0	+ 0	+ 0	+ 0	= 6,400	+ 75	+ 0	+ 22,237
a)	+250					=		+250	
b)	−100					= −100			
c)	−200			+ 200		= 0			
d)	−300				+ 300	= 0			
e)	+325							+325	
f)	−45	+ 45				= 0			
g)	−75					=	−75		
h)	−40		+ 40			= 0			

Total	$527 + $28,000	+ $45	+ $40	+ $200	+ $300	= 6,300	+ 0	+ 575	+ $22,237
	$29,112					= $29,112			

2-2

Cash	902.00
Accounts Receivable	425.00
Delivery Equipment	12,000.00
Supplies	160.00
Tucker, Drawing	600.00
Advertising Expense	95.00
Telephone Expense	140.00
Trucking Expense	150.00
Accounts Payable	1,075.00
Tucker, Capital	12,297.00
Delivery Income	1,100.00

THINK IT OVER

Separate each store's bookkeeping records to determine how profitable each one is.

Chapter 3

QUESTIONS

1. at least 500 postings to ledger accounts—a minimum of two accounts per transaction

2. Dates of entries are needed for each transaction to follow logically.

3. debits entered first, next to date column
    credits entered on next line, indented

4. (a) true
    (b) false

5. A transaction may result in two increases (example: buying supplies on credit) or two decreases (example: paying cash for a liability).

6. Assets have debit balances.

PROBLEMS

3-1

		JOURNAL			*Page 7*

Date		Account Title	PR	Debit	Credit
20__ Oct.	2	Salary Expense		175 00	
		Cash			175 00
		Employee's Salary			
	7	Cash		600 00	
		Design Income			600 00
		Received for a design			
	14	Supplies		200 00	
		Cash			200 00
		Supplies and Material			
	16	Cash		1000 00	
		Notes Payable—Vernon Trust Co.			1000 00
		Borrowed from bank			
	21	Cash		500 00	
		Design Income			500 00
		Received for a design			
	23	Equipment		360 00	
		Cash			160 00
		Accounts Payable—Textile Equipment Co.			200 00
		new drawing table			
	30	Rose Klein, Drawing		400 00	
		Cash			400 00
		Withdrawal			
	31	Cash		100 00	
		Accounts Receivable—Mary Wu			100 00
		Received on account			

3-2 October   2—Check stub
                7—check received
                14—check stub and/or seller's receipt
                16—bank loan form
                21—sales invoice
                23—statement and receipt from Textile Equipment Co.
                30—check stub
                31—check received

3-3 (1)

Cash	Equipment	Supplies
1,245	3,670	430

Accounts Payable—L.D. Brown	Accounts Payable—J.C. Tucker	Emilee Suzanne, Cap.
400	175	4,770

3-3 (2) Total Assets, $5,345

Total Liabilities $ 575
Capital   4,770
Total Liab. + OE $ 5,345

Therefore:

Emilee Suzanne, Capital
4,770

3-4 (1)

Cash		A/R—D. R. Able		A/R—M. O. Jackson	
1,305		150		225	

A/R—V. L. Witten		Truck		Supplies	
85		15,750		395	

A/P—City Trust		A/P—H&H Mfg.		Paul Jacobs, Capital	
	1,250		800		15,860

3-4 (2) Total Assets, $17,910

Total Liabilities	$ 2,050
Capital	15,860
Total Liab. + OE	$17,910

3-5

Cash				Equipment		
	4,075	*Ex.*	150		12,500	
(2)	1,000	(1)	75	(4)	500	
(3)	2,500					

Supplies			Notes Payable			
	200		*Ex.*	150		2,000
(1)	75				(2)	1,000

Accounts Payable			Kimberley Travis, Capital		
	(4)	500			14,775
				(3)	2,500

3-6

Trans. No.	Assets	Liabilities	Owner's Equity
Example	Decrease	Decrease	
(1)	No change		
(2)	Increase	Increase	
(3)	Increase		Increase
(4)	Increase	Increase	

3-7 (1) and (2)

Cash		A/R—H. L. Rhodes MD		A/R—Mary Turner MD	
437.50	(b) 65.00	50.00	(a) 50.00	50.00	(e) 25.00
(a) 50.00	(c) 75.00				
(d) 500.00					
(e) 25.00					
1,012.50	140	– 0 –		25.00	
872.50					

H/R—T. W. Vine DDS		Equipment		Supplies	
35.00		2,650.00		25.00	
				(c) 75.00	
				100.00	

A/P—State Telephone Co.		A/P—Ace Electricians		Lori Luing, Capital	
	215.00	(b) 65.00	65.00		2,967.50
					(d) 500.00
			– 0 –		3,467.50

3-7 (3) Total Assets $3,682.50

Total Liabilities	$ 215.00
Capital	3,467.50
Total Liab. + OE	$ 3,682.50

THINK IT OVER

Reasons for being in business:

(1) to be successful

(2) to make a profit

(3) to serve a useful purpose

The profit motive combines (1) and (2) above.

Chapter 4

QUESTIONS

1. Steps in posting journal entries:
   (1) For the account debited, enter the amount on the debit side of the account.
   (2) Enter the year, month, and day in the date column (do not repeat the year or month).
   (3) Enter the journal page number in the posting reference column of the account.
   (4) Enter the account number in the posting reference column of the journal.

2. (a) Journal posting refers to the account.
   (b) Account posting refers to the journal page.

3. A clerk resumes posting work after the last account posting indicated in the journal PR column.

4. A trial balance "in balance" proves that debit and credit column totals are equal.

5. To locate an error in the trial balance:
   (a) Total columns, re-add.
   (b) Verify that each account is properly listed as a debit or a credit.
   (c) Verify correct postings from journal to accounts.
   (d) Verify correct account balances.

6. Any of the above done incorrectly will cause a trial balance to be "out of balance."

7. Errors that will not cause a trial balance to be out of balance include
   (a) omitting an entire entry.
   (b) posting to an incorrect account—a debit to a debit, or a credit to a credit.
   (c) posting an incorrect amount to both a debit and a credit.
   (d) posting a transaction twice.

PROBLEMS

4-1

Account No. 11
Cash

Date		Explanation	PR	Debit	Credit	Balance
Oct.	10		G6	2500		2500
	18		G6		500	2000
	25				250	1750

Account No. 12
Equipment

Date		Explanation	PR	Debit	Credit	Balance
Oct.	1		G6	1000		1000

Account No. 21
Accounts Payable

Date		Explanation	PR	Debit	Credit	Balance
Oct.	1		G6		1000	1000
	25		G6	250		750

Account No. 32
Berger, Drawing

Date		Explanation	PR	Debit	Credit	Balance
Oct.	18		G6	500		500

Account No. 41
Service Income

Date		Explanation	PR	Debit	Credit	Balance
Oct.	10		G6		2500	2500

GENERAL JOURNAL   Page 6

Date		Accounts	PR	Debit	Credit
20__					
Oct.	1	Equipment	12	1000 00	
		Accounts Payable—Landers Mfg. Co.	21		1000 00
		5 Motors, Voucher No. 31			
	10	Cash	11	2500 00	
		Service Income	41		2500 00
		Receipts Nos. 1–35, to date			
	18	L. D. Berger, Drawing	32	500 00	
		Cash	11		500 00
		Withdrawal, Personal Use,			
		Check No. 57			
	25	Accounts Payable—Landers Mfg. Co.	21	250 00	
		Cash	11		250 00
		Partial Payment, Check No. 58			

4-2

Alan Korn, Consulting
TRIAL BALANCE

		DEBITS	CREDITS
(1) and (2)	Cash	$ 2,020.00	
	Equipment	3,965.00	
	Supplies	60.00	
	Korn, Drawing	500.00	
	Advertising Expense	100.00	
	Utilities Expense	50.00	
	Accounts Payable		2,390.00
	Korn, Capital		3,060.00
	Services Income		1,245.00
	Totals	$6,695.00	$6,695.00

4–3 (1) and (2)

GENERAL JOURNAL   Page 3

Date		Account Title	PR	Debit	Credit
20__					
Oct.	2	Supplies	13	1 2 5 00	
		Cash	11		1 2 5 00
	7	Cash	11	2 0 0 00	
		Fee Income	41		2 0 0 00
	11	Note Payable	21	5 0 00	
		Cash	11		5 0 00
	21	Cash	11	2 4 0 00	
		Fee Income	41		2 4 0 00
	27	Miscellaneous Expense	51	6 5 00	
		Cash	11		6 5 00
	31	Anita Schaffer, Drawing	32	3 0 0 00	
		Cash	11		3 0 0 00

4-3 (2)

GENERAL LEDGER

Account No. 11
Cash

Date		Explanation	PR	Debit	Credit	Balance
20__ Oct.	1	Balance	✓			1375
	2		G3		125	1250
	7		G3	200		1450
	11		G3		50	1400
	21		G3	240		1640
	27		G3		65	1575
	31		G3		300	1275

Account No. 12
Equipment

Date		Explanation	PR	Debit	Credit	Balance
20__ Oct.	1	Balance	✓			1642.50

Account No. 13
Supplies

Date		Explanation	PR	Debit	Credit	Balance
20__ Oct.	1	Balance	✓			230
	2		G3	125		355

Account No. 21
Note Payable

Date		Explanation	PR	Debit	Credit	Balance
20__ Oct.	1	Balance	✓			875
	11		G3	50		825

Account No. 31
Anita Schaffer, Capital

Date		Explanation	PR	Debit	Credit	Balance
20__ Oct.	1	Balance	✓			2372.50

Account No. 32
Anita Schaffer, Drawing

Date		Explanation	PR	Debit	Credit	Balance
20__ Oct.	31		G3	300		300

Account No. 41
Fee Income

Date		Explanation	PR	Debit	Credit	Balance
20__ Oct.	7		G3		200	200
	21		G3		240	440

Account No. 51
Miscellaneous Expense

Date		Explanation	PR	Debit	Credit	Balance
20__ Oct.	27		G3	65		65

4-3 (3)

Anita Schaffer

Trial Balance

October 31, 20__

		Debit	Credit
Cash		1275 00	
Equipment		1642 50	
Supplies		355 00	
Anita Schaffer, Capital			2372 50
Anita Schaffer, Drawing		300 00	
Note Payable			825 00
Fee Income			440 00
Miscellaneous Expense		65 00	
Totals		3637 50	3637 50

4-4

T.R. Price, Carpenter

Trial Balance

November 30, 20__

Cash		2645 00		
Equipment		1500 00		
Truck		7500 00		
Accounts Payable			55 00	
T.R. Price, Capital			10570 00	
T.R. Price, Drawing		500 00		
Commissions Income			1650 00	
Advertising Expense		100 00		
Rent Expense		175 00		
Salary Expense		300 00		
Miscellaneous Expense		50 00		
Totals		$12770 00	$12770 00	

4-5 (1)
Accounts Payable ($600.00) should go in the Credit column.

4-5 (2)
Trial Balance totals, $7,251.40

4-6 (1) Service Income ($1,875.50) should go in the Credit column.

THINK IT OVER

1. Fowler should retrace the steps in the procedure:
    1) check trial balance column totals
    2) verify that accounts are entered in proper debit or credit column
    3) verify correct account balances
    4) check posting procedure for each entry
    5) verify proper journal entry

2. Jacobs neglected to journalize and post an entry for the same amount—$50—thus not affecting the equality of debits and credits in the trial balance.

3. Another error might be posting a debit or credit to an incorrect account—a debit to Supplies, for example, instead of to Equipment.

4. The $100 error overstates the credit total by $100 and understates the debit total by $100. The transposed error understates the debit total by $9 ($54 – $45). The difference is $209 ($200 + $9).

Chapter 5

QUESTIONS

1. The revenue recognition principle and the matching principle.

2. The amount of the supplies adjustment is the amount of supplies used by the business during a period of time

3. To report the amount of expense that has been used up.

PROBLEMS

5-1

Jun.	30	Supplies Expense			1 0 0 00		
		Supplies				1 0 0 00
Jun.	30	Insurance Expense			5 0 00		
		Prepaid Insurance				5 0 00
Jun.	30	Salaries Expense			5 0 0 00		
		Salaries Payable				5 0 0 00

5-2 (a)

Jan.	31	Supplies Expense	55	1 2 0 00	
		Supplies	14		1 2 0 00
Jan.	31	Insurance Expense	52	5 0 00	
		Prepaid Insurance	15		5 0 00
Jan.	31	Accounts Receivable	12	5 0 0 00	
		Legal Fees Earned	41		5 0 0 00
Jan.	31	Advertising Expense	51	2 5 0 00	
		Accounts Payable	21		2 5 0 00

5-2 (b)

Cash   No. 11

Date			PR	Dr.	Cr.	Balance
20__ Jan.	1	Balance	✓			1500 00
	31		G3	3650 00		5150 00
	31		G3		1790 00	3360 00

Accounts Receivable   No. 12

Date			PR	Dr.	Cr.	Balance
20__ Jan.	1	Balance	✓			500 00
	31		G3	3200 00		3700 00
	31		G3		150 00	3550 00
	31		G3		35 00	3515 00
	31	Adjustment	G6	500 00		4015 00

Supplies   No. 14

Date			PR	Dr.	Cr.	Balance
20__ Jan.	1	Balance	✓			275 00
	3		G1	50 00		325 00
	31	Adjustment	G6		120 00	205 00

Prepaid Insurance   No. 15

Date			PR	Dr.	Cr.	Balance
20__ Jan.	1	Balance	✓			300 00
	31	Adjustment	G6		50 00	250 00

Accounts Payable   No. 21

Date			PR	Dr.	Cr.	Balance
20__ Jan.	1	Balance	✓			1000 00
	31		G3		1200 00	2200 00
	31		G3	400 00		1800 00
	31	Adjustment	G6		250 00	2050 00

Timothy Sullivan, Capital   No. 31

Date			PR	Dr.	Cr.	Balance
20__ Jan.	1	Balance	✓			5375 00
	10		G2		2500 00	7875 00

Timothy Sullivan, Drawing   No. 32

Date			PR	Dr.	Cr.	Balance
20__ Jan.	15		G2	150 00		150 00
	30		G3	150 00		300 00

Legal Fees Earned   No. 41

Date			PR	Dr.	Cr.	Balance
20__ Jan.	31		G3		3200 00	3200 00
	31		G3		1000 00	4200 00
	31	Adjustment	G6		500 00	4700 00

Advertising Expense   No. 51

Date			PR	Dr.	Cr.	Balance
20__						
Jan.	3		G1	1 0 0 00		1 0 0 00
	31	Adjustment	G6	2 5 0 00		3 5 0 00

Insurance Expense   No. 52

Date			PR	Dr.	Cr.	Balance
Jan.	31	Adjustment	G6	5 0 00		5 0 00

Miscellaneous Expense   No. 53

Date			PR	Dr.	Cr.	Balance
20__						
Jan.	12		G2	2 5 00		2 5 00
	27		G3	1 5 00		4 0 00

Rent Expense   No. 54

Date			PR	Dr.	Cr.	Balance
20__						
Jan.	2		G1	4 0 0 00		4 0 0 00

Supplies Expense   No. 55

Date			PR	Dr.	Cr.	Balance
Jan.	31	Adjustment	G6	1 2 0 00		1 2 0 00

Chapter 6

QUESTIONS

1. Who? What? When?

2. 30 days—April, June, September, November
   31 days—January, March, May, July, August, October, December
   28 or 29 Days—February

3. July 1—September 30
   January 1—March 31
   October 1—December 31

4. Assets = Liabilities + Owner's Equity

5. Assets – Liabilities = Owner's Equity

6. Income statements are prepared first, followed by owner's equity statements and finally, a balance sheet.

7. Owner's equity will increase by additional investments and net income.

8. Owner's equity will decrease by a withdrawal and a net loss.

9. The date on an income statement and an owner's equity statement indicates the fiscal period. The date on a balance sheet indicates the last day of the fiscal period.

10. An income statement describes how a business operates—its income, costs, and expenses resulting in a net income or a net loss. An owner's equity statement describes changes in the owner's capital account. A balance sheet describes the financial condition of a business at the end of a fiscal period—its assets, liabilities, and owner's equity.

11. A net income results when total income is greater than total expenses. If expenses are greater than net income, the result is a net loss.

12. A report form balance sheet lists assets, liabilities, and owner's equity in a vertical arrangement; the account form lists assets on the left side with liabilities and owner's equity on the right side (similar to a T-account).

PROBLEMS

6-1

Left Side	Right Side
1. Asset	
2.	Liability
3. Asset	
4.	Liability
5. Asset	
6. Asset	
7. Asset	
8.	Owner's equity
9. Asset	
10.	Owner's equity

6-2

Maria's Beauty Salon

Balance Sheet

August 31, 20___

Assets		Liabilities	
Cash	1750 00	Accounts Payable	2775 00
Furn. & Fixtures	8900 00	Total Liabilities	2775 00
Beauty Supplies	600 00		
		Owner's Equity	
		Maria Lopez, Capital	8475 00
Total Assets	11250 00	Total Liab. & OE	11250 00

6-3

Lady Cake Bake Shoppe

Balance Sheet

July 31, 20___

Assets		Liabilities	
Cash	1250 00	Accounts Payable	535 00
Supplies	180 00	Notes Payable	2357 500
Building	6850 00	Total Liabilities	2892 500
Bakery Equipment	2620 00	Owner's Equity	
Furniture & Fixtures	630 00	Mueller, Capital	7512 500
Total Assets	10405 00	Total Liabilities & O.E.	10405 00

6-4 (a)

T. R. Price

Income Statement

For Month Ended November 30, 20___

Revenue:		
Commissions Income		1650 00
Expenses:		
Advertising Expense	100 00	
Miscellaneous Expense	50 00	
Rent Expense	175 00	
Salary Expense	300 00	
Total Expenses		625 00
Net Income		1025 00

6-4 (b)

T. R. Price

Owner's Equity Statement

For Month Ended November 30, 20__

Beginning Capital, Nov. 1, 20__			10570 00
Plus: Net Income		1025 00	
Less: Withdrawals		500 00	
Net Increase in Capital			525 00
Ending Capital, Nov. 30, 20__			11095 00

6-4 (c)

T. R. Price

Balance Sheet

November 30, 20__

Assets		Liabilities	
Cash	2645 00	Accounts Payable	550 00
Equipment	1500 00	Owner's Equity	
Truck	7500 00	T. R. Price, Capital	11095 00
Total Assets	11645 00	Total Liab. & OE	11645 00

6-5 (a)

Danziger Designs

Income Statement

For the Month Ending Sept. 30, 20___

Revenue:			
Fee Income			2 4 0 0 00
Expenses:			
Advertising Expense		1 6 0 00	
Insurance Expense		4 0 00	
Materials Expense		1 0 0 00	
Rent Expense		2 5 0 00	
Salary Expense		4 0 0 00	
Total Expenses			9 5 0 00
Net Income			1 4 5 0 00

6-5 (b)

Danziger Designs

Owner's Equity Statement

For the Month Ending Sept. 30, 20___

Beginning Capital, Sept. 1, 20___			4 2 5 1 40
Add: Net Income		1 4 5 0 00	
Less: Withdrawal		8 0 0 00	
Net Increase in Capital			6 5 0 00
Ending Capital, Sept. 30, 20___			4 9 0 1 40

6-5 (c)

Danziger Designs

Balance Sheet

September 30, 20___

Assets		Liabilities	
Cash	1762 50	Accounts Payable	600 00
Accounts Receivable	738 90	Owner's Equity	
Equipment	2605 00	Ann Danziger, Capital	4901 40
Supplies	395 00		
Total Assets	5501 40	Total Liab. & OE	5501 40

6-6 (a)

Gayle's Reliable Service

Income Statement

For Month Ended October 31, 20___

Revenue:		
Service Income		1875 50
Expenses:		
Advertising Expense	200 00	
Auto Expense	400 00	
Miscellaneous Expense	50 00	
Telephone Expense	75 00	
Total Expenses		725 00
Net Income		1150 50

6-6 (b)

Gayle's Reliable Service

Owner's Equity Statement

For Month Ended October 31, 20__

Beginning Capital, Oct. 1, 20__			6 3 0 2 00
Plus: Net Income		1 1 5 0 50	
Less: Withdrawals		6 0 0 00	
Net Increase in Capital			5 5 0 50
Ending Capital, Oct. 31, 20__			6 8 5 2 50

6-6 (c)

Gayle's Reliable Service

Balance Sheet

October 31, 20__

Assets		*Liabilities*	
Cash	7 6 0 00	*Note Payable*	3 6 0 0 00
Accounts Receivable	1 4 2 50	*Owner's Equity*	
Automobile	9 2 0 0 00	*Rebecca Gayle, Capital*	6 8 5 2 50
Supplies	3 5 0 00		
Total Assets	1 0 4 5 2 50	*Total Liab. & OE*	1 0 4 5 2 50

6-7 (a)

GENERAL JOURNAL   *Page 5*

Date		Description	PR	Debit	Credit
Jul.	*1*	*Cash*	*11*	8 0 0 0 00	
		Brown, Capital	*31*		8 0 0 0 00
Jul.	*2*	*Prepaid Rent*	*13*	3 6 0 0 00	
		Cash	*11*		3 6 0 0 00
Jul.	*2*	*Office Supplies*	*14*	2 0 0 00	
		Accounts Payable	*21*		2 0 0 00
Jul.	*5*	*Equipment*	*15*	8 0 0 00	
		Furniture	*16*	5 0 0 00	
		Cash	*11*		1 3 0 0 00
Jul.	*7*	*Accounts Receivable*	*12*	1 2 0 0 00	
		Design Income	*41*		1 2 0 0 00
Jul.	*12*	*Cash*	*11*	4 0 0 00	
		Design Income	*41*		4 0 0 00
Jul.	*20*	*Accounts Payable*	*21*	2 0 0 00	
		Cash	*11*		2 0 0 00
Jul.	*23*	*Cash*	*11*	6 0 0 00	
		Accounts Receivable	*12*		6 0 0 00
Jul.	*25*	*Advertising Expense*	*51*	2 0 0 00	
		Cash	*11*		2 0 0 00
Jul.	*28*	*Cash*	*11*	5 0 0 00	
		Unearned Design Fees	*22*		5 0 0 00
Jul.	*29*	*Cash*	*11*	6 0 0 00	
		Accounts Receivable	*12*		6 0 0 00

6-7 (b) and (d)

GENERAL LEDGER

Account No. 11
Cash

Date		Explanation	PR	Debit	Credit	Balance
Jul.	1		G5	800000		800000
Jul.	2		G5		360000	440000
Jul.	5		G5		130000	310000
Jul.	12		G5	40000		350000
Jul.	20		G5		20000	330000
Jul.	23		G5	60000		390000
Jul.	25		G5		20000	370000
Jul.	28		G5	50000		420000
Jul.	29		G5	60000		480000

Account No. 12
Accounts Receivable

Date		Explanation	PR	Debit	Credit	Balance
Jul.	7		G5	120000		120000
Jul.	23		G5		60000	60000
Jul.	29		G5		60000	—0—
Jul.	31	Adjustment	G5	30000		30000

Account No. 13
Prepaid Rent

Date		Explanation	PR	Debit	Credit	Balance
Jul.	2		G5	360000		360000
Jul.	31	Adjustment	G5		60000	300000

Account No. 14
Office Supplies

Date		Explanation	PR	Debit	Credit	Balance
Jul.	2		G5	20000		20000
Jul.	31	Adjustment	G5		7500	12500

Account No. 15
Equipment

Date		Explanation	PR	Debit	Credit	Balance
Jul.	5		G5	80000		80000

Account No. 16
Furniture

Date		Explanation	PR	Debit	Credit	Balance
Jul.	5		G5	500 00		500 00

Account No. 21
Accounts Payable

Date		Explanation	PR	Debit	Credit	Balance
Jul.	2		G5		200 00	200 00
Jul.	20		G5	200 00		–0–
Jul.	31	Adjustment	G5		50 00	50 00

Account No. 22
Unearned Design Fees

Date		Explanation	PR	Debit	Credit	Balance
Jul.	28		G5		500 00	500 00

Account No. 31
Brown, Capital

Date		Explanation	PR	Debit	Credit	Balance
Jul.	1		G5		8000 00	8000 00

Account No. 41
Design Income

Date		Explanation	PR	Debit	Credit	Balance
Jul.	7		G5		1200 00	1200 00
Jul.	12		G5		400 00	1600 00
Jul.	31	Adjustment	G5		300 00	1900 00

Account No. 51
Advertising Expense

Date		Explanation	PR	Debit	Credit	Balance
Jul.	25		G5	200 00		200 00

Account No. 52
Office Supplies Expense

Date		Explanation	PR	Debit	Credit	Balance
Jul.	31	Adjustment	G5	75 00		75 00

Account No. 53
Telephone Expense

Date		Explanation	PR	Debit	Credit	Balance
Jul.	31	Adjustment	G5	5000		5000

Account No. 54
Rent Expense

Date		Explanation	PR	Debit	Credit	Balance
Jul.	31	Adjustment	G5	60000		60000

6-7 (c)

Brown Consulting

Trial Balance

July 31, 20__

	Debit	Credit
Cash	480000	
Accounts Receivable	—0—	
Prepaid Rent	360000	
Office Supplies	20000	
Equipment	80000	
Furniture	50000	
Accounts Payable		—0—
Unearned Design Fees		50000
Brown, Capital		800000
Design Income		160000
Advertising Expense	20000	
Totals	1010000	1010000

6-7 (d)

General Journal

Adjusting Entries

Date			Description	PR	Debit	Credit
Jul.	31		Office Supplies Expense	52	7500	
			Office Supplies	14		7500
	31		Accounts Receivable	12	30000	
			Design Income	41		30000
	31		Telephone Expense	53	5000	
			Accounts Payable	21		5000
	31		Rent Expense	54	60000	
			Prepaid Rent	13		60000

6-7 (e)

Brown Consulting

Adjusted Trial Balance

July 31, 20__

Cash	4800 00	
Accounts Receivable	300 00	
Prepaid Rent	3000 00	
Office Supplies	125 00	
Equipment	800 00	
Furniture	500 00	
Accounts Payable		50 00
Unearned Design Fees		500 00
Brown, Capital		8000 00
Design Income		1900 00
Advertising Expense	200 00	
Office Supplies Expense	75 00	
Telephone Expense	50 00	
Rent Expense	600 00	
Totals	10450 00	10450 00

6-7 (f)

Brown Consulting
Income Statement
For month ended July 31, 20__

Revenues:			
Design Income			1900 00
Expenses:			
Advertising	200 00		
Office Supplies	75 00		
Telephone	50 00		
Rent	600 00		
Total Expenses		925 00	
Net Income		975 00	

Brown Consulting
Owner's Equity Statement
For month ended July 31, 20__

Brown, Capital, July 1			—0—
add:			
Net income	975 00		
Investment	8000 00		
Increase in Capital		8975 00	
Brown, Capital, July 31		8975 00	

Brown Consulting
Balance Sheet
July 31, 20__

Assets:		Liabilities:	
Cash	4800 00	Accounts Payable	50 00
Accounts Receivable	300 00	Unearned Design Fees	500 00
Prepaid Rent	3000 00	Total Liabilities	550 00
Office Supplies	125 00		
Furniture	800 00	Owner's Equity:	
Equipment	500 00	Brown, Capital	8975 00
Total Assets	9525 00	Total Liabilities & O.E.	9525 00

THINK IT OVER

1. Answers will vary for each person.

2. A Balance Sheet is a "picture" at a given moment, a specific date—June 30 or December 31. An Income Statement shows activity over a period of time, for the period ending December 31, for example.

Chapter 7

QUESTIONS

1. Net increases and/or decreases are transferred to the capital account by recording and posting closing entries.

2. Closing entries in correct order:
   (a) income accounts
   (b) expense accounts
   (c) net income or net loss
   (d) the drawing account

3. A credit balance in the Income Summary account indicates a net income.

4. Debit the owner's Capital account, credit Income Summary.

5. The first closing entry zeros out the revenue accounts.

6. The second closing entry zeros out the expense accounts.

7. The third closing entry zeros out the Income Summary account for either a net income (debit Income Summary, credit Capital) or for a net loss (debit Capital, credit Income Summary).

8. The fourth closing entry zeros out the Drawing account (debit, Capital, credit Drawing).

9. The third closing entry transfers the net income or net loss to owner's equity.

10. The fourth closing entry subtracts the Drawing account balance from owner's equity.

11. After closing entries have been posted, all income and expense accounts and drawing accounts have been zeroed out.

12. Post-closing trial balance proves the equality of debits and credits in general ledger accounts which remain open.

PROBLEMS

7-1   Net Income, $3,350 (Revenues, $4,250 Less Expenses, $900)

			Closing Entries					
20__ Dec.	31		Consulting Fees Income			375000		
			Royalty Income			50000		
			Income Summary					425000
	31		Income Summary			90000		
			Advertising Expense					10000
			Miscellaneous Expense					6000
			Rent Expense					25000
			Salary Expense					40000
			Telephone Expense					9000
	31		Income Summary			335000		
			Gwen Vreeland, Capital					335000
	31		Gwen Vreeland, Capital			180000		
			Gwen Vreeland, Drawing					180000

7-2

(1)
Allen Insurance Agency
Trial Balance
November 30, 20___

	Debit	Credit
Cash	$2,800.00	
Accounts Receivable	3,895.00	
Equipment	4,000.00	
Automobile	12,500.00	
Supplies	750.00	
Accounts Payable		6,000.00
Elliot Allen, Capital		12,920.00
Elliot Allen, Drawing	1,500.00	
Commissions Income		8,500.00
Automobile Expense	600.00	
Office Expense	175.00	
Rent Expense	300.00	
Salary Expense	900.00	
Totals	$27,420.00	$27,420.00

(2)   Net Income $6,525.00   (8,500.00 – 600.00 – 175.00 – 300.00 – 900.00)

7-2 (3)

			Closing Entries						
20__									
Nov.	30		Commissions Income			850000			
			Income Summary					850000	
	30		Income Summary			197500			
			Automobile Expense					60000	
			Office Expense					17500	
			Rent Expense					30000	
			Salary Expense					90000	
	30		Income Summary			652500			
			Elliot Allen, Capital					652500	
	30		Elliot Allen, Capital			150000			
			Elliot Allen, Drawing					150000	

7-3 (1a)

Earl Alpert, Esquire

Income Statement

For the Quarter Ended June 30, 20__

Revenue					
Legal Fees Income				950000	
Expenses:					
Miscellaneous Expense			15000		
Office Expense			22500		
Rent Expense			120000		
Salary Expense			300000		
Travel Expense			7500		
Total Expenses				465000	
Net Income				485000	

7-3 (1b)

Earl Alpert, Esquire				
Owner's Equity Statement				
June 30, 20__				
Beginning Capital: April 1, 2010				2330075
Plus: Additional Investment			100000	
Net Income			485000	
Increase in Capital			585000	
Less: Withdrawals			480000	
Net Increase in Capital				105000
Ending Capital, June 30, 20__				2435075

7-3 (1c)

Earl Alpert, Esquire		
Balance Sheet		
June 30, 20__		

Assets		Liabilities	
Cash	160500	Accts. Payable	187500
Accounts Receivable	1458000	Owner's Equity	
Office Equipment	396000	Earl Alpert, Capital	2435075
Furniture	525000		
Supplies	83075		
Total Assets	2622575	Total Liability & OE	2622575

278 Answer Key

7-3 (2)

			Closing Entries					
20__ June	30		Income Summary			9 50 0 00		
			Legal Fees Income					9 50 0 00
	30		Miscellaneous Expense			1 50 00		
			Office Expense			2 25 00		
			Rent Expense			1 2 0 0 00		
			Salary Expense			3 0 0 0 00		
			Telephone Expense			7 5 00		
			Income Summary					4 65 0 00
	30		Income Summary			4 85 0 00		
			Earl Alpert, Capital					4 85 0 00
	30		Earl Alpert, Capital			4 80 0 00		
			Earl Alpert, Drawing					4 80 0 00

7-4 (1a)

Pamela Washington

Income Statement

For the Month Ended December 31, 20__

Revenue:				
Fees Income				1 85 0 00
Expenses:				
Automobile Expense		9 0 00		
Office Expense		1 0 0 00		
Rent Expense		1 7 5 00		
Total Expenses				3 65 00
Net Income				1 48 5 00

7-4 (1b)

Pamela Washington

Owner's Equity Statement

For the Month Ended December 31, 20__

Beginning Capital, Dec. 1			6630 00
Plus: Net Income		1485 00	
Less: Withdrawal		800 00	
Net Increase in Capital			685 00
Ending Capital, Dec. 31			7315 00

7-4 (1c)

Pamela Washington

Balance Sheet

December 31, 20__

Assets		Liabilities	
Cash	2185 00	Accounts Payable	1700 00
Accounts Receivable	1250 00	Owner's Equity	
Equipment	5000 00	Pamela Washington,	
Supplies	580 00	Capital	7315 00
Total Assets	9015 00	Total Liabilities & OE	9015 00

7-4 (2) and (3)

Account No. 11   **GENERAL LEDGER**
Cash

Date	Explanation	PR	Debit	Credit	Balance
	Balance				2185 00

Account No. 12
Accounts Receivable

Date	Explanation	PR	Debit	Credit	Balance
	Balance				1250 00

Account No. 13
Equipment

Date	Explanation	PR	Debit	Credit	Balance
	Balance				5000 00

Account No. 14
Supplies

Date	Explanation	PR	Debit	Credit	Balance
	Balance				580 00

Account No. 21
Accounts Payable

Date	Explanation	PR	Debit	Credit	Balance
	Balance				1700 00

Account No. 31
Washington, Capital

Date		Explanation	PR	Debit	Credit	Balance
		Balance				6630 00
Dec.	31	Closing			1485 00	8115 00
Dec.	31	Closing		800 00		7315 00

Account No. 32
Washington, Drawing

Date		Explanation	PR	Debit	Credit	Balance
		Balance				800 00
Dec.	31	Closing			800 00	–0–

Account No. 35
Income Summary

Date		Explanation	PR	Debit	Credit	Balance
Dec	31	Closing			1850 00	1850 00
Dec	31	Closing		365 00		1485 00
Dec	31	Closing		1485 00		-0-

Account No. 41
Fees Income

Date		Explanation	PR	Debit	Credit	Balance
		Balance				1850 00
Dec	31	Closing		1850 00		-0-

Account No. 51
Automobile Expense

Date		Explanation	PR	Debit	Credit	Balance
		Balance				90 00
Dec	31	Closing			90 00	-0-

Account No. 52
Office Expense

Date		Explanation	PR	Debit	Credit	Balance
		Balance				100 00
Dec	31	Closing			100 00	-0-

Account No. 53
Rent Expense

Date		Explanation	PR	Debit	Credit	Balance
		Balance				175 00
Dec	31	Closing			175 00	-0-

7-4 (3)

	GENERAL JOURNAL			Page 7

Date			Account Title	PR	Debit	Credit
20__						
Dec.	31		Closing Entries			
			Fees Income	41	1 85000	
			Income Summary	35		1 85000
	31		Income Summary	35	36500	
			Automobile Expense	51		9000
			Office Expense	52		10000
			Rent Expense	53		17500
	31		Income Summary	35	1 48500	
			Washington, Capital	31		1 48500
	31		Washington, Capital	31	80000	
			Washington, Drawing	32		80000

7-4 (4)

Pamela Washington

Post-Closing Trial Balance

December 31, 20__

		Debit	Credit
Cash		2 18500	
Accounts Receivable		1 25000	
Equipment		5 00000	
Supplies		58000	
Accounts Payable			1 70000
Pamela Washington, Capital			7 31500
Totals		9 01500	9 01500

THINK IT OVER

Green will mix financial records and be unable to determine his profit or loss for a given fiscal period. IRS will not accept these mixed records. He will have to reexamine his work to separate one period from the next in order to prepare acceptable tax returns.

PART ONE EXAMINATION

PART I

1.	T	11.	T
2.	F	12.	T
3.	T	13.	F
4.	T	14.	T
5.	F	15.	F
6.	T	16.	T
7.	T	17.	F
8.	F	18.	T
9.	F	19.	F
10.	F	20.	F

PART II

1.	G	9.	M
2.	K	10.	D
3.	Q	11.	B
4.	S	12.	O
5.	F	13.	A
6.	N	14.	J
7.	H	15.	E
8.	R	16.	T

PART III

	Account Dr.	Account Cr.
1.	J	A
2.	B	A
3.	A	D
4.	G	F
5.	B	A, C
6.	E	A
7.	F	H, I, J
8.	F	D
9.	D	F
10.	D	E

PART IV

Country-Wide Plumbing

Income Statement

For the year ended December 31, 20__

Revenues:			
Fees Income			18620 00
Expenses:			
Advertising Expense		480 00	
Automobile Expense		2400 00	
Miscellaneous Expense		120 00	
Rent Expense		3600 00	
Telephone Expense		1200 00	
Total Expenses			7800 00
Net Income			10820 00

Part IV (2)

	Country-Wide Plumbing

Owner's Equity Statement

December 31, 20__

Beginning Capital, Jan 1, 20__			9685 00
Plus: Additional Investment		5000 00	
Net Income		10820 00	
Increase in Capital		15820 00	
Less: Withdrawals		9500 00	
Net Increase in Capital			6320 00
Ending Capital, Dec. 31, 20__			16005 00

Part IV (3)

Country-Wide Plumbing

Balance Sheet

December 31, 20__

Assets		Liabilities	
Cash	1497 50	Accounts Payable	970 00
Accounts Receivable	385 00		
Supplies	242 50	Owner's Equity	
Truck	14850 00	Chet Gorski, Capital	16005 00
Total Assets	16975 00	Total Liabilities & OE	16975 00

Part IV (4)

GENERAL JOURNAL

			Closing Entries				
20__ Dec.	31		Fees Income		18620 00		
			Income Summary				18620 00
	31		Income Summary		7800 00		
			Advertising Expense				480 00
			Automobile Expense				2400 00
			Miscellaneous Expense				120 00
			Rent Expense				3600 00
			Telephone Expense				1200 00
	31		Income Summary		10820 00		
			Chet Gorski, Capital				10820 00
	31		Chet Gorski, Capital		9500 00		
			Chet Gorski, Drawing				9500 00

Part V (1)

NO 207	$ 35.50					No. 207
DATE January 7 20						1-830 960
TO Wilson Supply Co.					January 7 20	
FOR Smoke Alarm						
(Equipment)						

	DOLLARS	CENTS
BAL. BRO'T FOR'D	382	47
AMT. DEPOSITED	225	00
TOTAL	607	47
AMT. THIS CHECK	35	50
BAL. CAR'D FOR'D	571	97

Pay to the order of Wilson Supply Company $ 35.50

Thirty-five and ———————— $\frac{50}{100}$ Dollars

BOLTON NATIONAL BANK
of New York, NY

Student's Name

⑈0860⋯0830⑈ 1248⋯671⑈

Part V (2)

JOURNAL

20__ Jan	7		Equipment		35 50		
			Cash				35 50
			Bought Smoke Alarm				

Chapter 8

QUESTIONS

1. Three parties to a check are the drawer, drawee, and payee.

2. A signature card is used by the drawer's bank (the drawee) to verify the drawer's handwritten name and signature.

3. The service charge entry should debit Miscellaneous Expense and credit Cash.

4. A bank reconciliation is prepared to bring together the checkbook balance and the bank statement balance because
    (a) omitted deposits (a deposit in transit) are not included on the bank statement.
    (b) outstanding checks are not on the bank statement.
    (c) bank service charges are not deducted in the checkbook until the bank statement is received.

5. One person handling the petty cash fund limits responsibility to just one person.

6. To establish the petty cash fund, draw a check payable to Petty Cash. To replenish the fund, draw a check payable to Cash. List on the check stub the amount spent on each expense with the replenishing check for the total spent.

7. The entry to establish Petty Cash should debit Petty Cash and credit Cash.

8. The entry to replenish the fund should debit each account for which petty cash was spent and credit the cash account.

9. Petty cash is proved by subtracting the sum of all petty cash vouchers from the original amount in the petty cash fund. The difference should equal the amount of cash remaining in the fund.

PROBLEMS

8-1

		DOLLARS	CENTS
CASH		1049	00
COINS		8	72
CHECKS		148	65
		79	15
TOTAL ITEMS TOTAL		1285	52

8-2 (1)

NO	118	$ 40.00		
DATE	Jan. 15		20	
TO	K–Mart			
FOR	Cleaning supplies			

	DOLLARS	CENTS
BAL. BRO'T FOR'D	136	50
AMT. DEPOSITED		
TOTAL		
AMT. THIS CHECK	40	00
BAL. CAR'D FOR'D	96	50

No. 118

1-830
860

January 15   20

Pay to the
order of   K–Mart $ 40.00

Forty and ——————————— $\frac{00}{100}$ Dollars

BOLTON NATIONAL BANK
of New York, NY   Jordan Glaser

⑆0860⋯0830⑆ 1848⋯671⑈

NO	119	$ 15.00		
DATE	Jan. 19		20	
TO	Brown's Cab			
FOR	Taxi service			

	DOLLARS	CENTS
BAL. BRO'T FOR'D	96	50
AMT. DEPOSITED		
TOTAL		
AMT. THIS CHECK	15	00
BAL. CAR'D FOR'D	81	50

No. 119

1-830
860

January 19   20

Pay to the
order of   Brown's Cab $ 15.00

Fifteen and ——————————— $\frac{00}{100}$ Dollars

BOLTON NATIONAL BANK
of New York, NY   Jordan Glaser

⑆0860⋯0830⑆ 1848⋯671⑈

NO	120	$ 50.00		
DATE	Jan. 22		20	
TO	Cash			
FOR	Personal			

	DOLLARS	CENTS
BAL. BRO'T FOR'D	81	50
AMT. DEPOSITED	175	00
TOTAL	256	50
AMT. THIS CHECK	50	00
BAL. CAR'D FOR'D	206	50

No. 120

1-830
860

January 22   20

Pay to the
order of   Cash $ 50.00

Fifty and ——————————— $\frac{00}{100}$ Dollars

BOLTON NATIONAL BANK
of New York, NY   Jordan Glaser

⑆0860⋯0830⑆ 1848⋯671⑈

8-2 (2)

FOR DEPOSIT TO THE ACCOUNT OF

		DOLLARS	CENTS
BILLS		75	00
COINS			
CHECKS AS FOLLOWS, PROPERLY ENDORSED		60	00
		40	00
TOTAL DEPOSIT		175	00

NAME _Jordan Glaser_

ADDRESS _5 Bolton Street_

DATE _Jan. 22_ 20 _____

BOLTON NATIONAL BANK
New York, NY

CHECKS AND OTHER ITEMS ARE RECEIVED FOR DEPOSIT SUBJECT TO
THE TERMS AND CONDITIONS OF THE BANKS COLLECTION AGREEMENT

⑈0860⋯0830⑈ 1848⋯671⋯

8-3

Checkbook Balance	420.90	Bank Balance		397.40
		Add: Deposit in transit		250.00
				647.40
Deduct: Service Charge	4.00	Deduct: Outstanding checks		
		#217 —	75.00	
		219 —	105.50	
		220 —	50.00	
				230.50
Adjusted checkbook balance	416.90	Adjusted Bank Balance		416.90

8-4 (1)

Bank Reconciliation				
Checkbook Balance	708.92	Bank Balance		626.66
		Add: Deposit in transit		375.00
				1,001.66
Deduct: Service Charge	3.60	Deduct: Outstanding checks		
		#641 —	92.50	
		644 —	107.25	
		646 —	37.80	
		647 —	58.79	
				296.34
Adjusted checkbook balance	705.32	Adjusted Bank Balance		705.32

8-4 (2)

20__								
Jan.	31	Miscellaneous Expense			3 60		
		Cash					3 60
		Bank Service Charge, Jan.					

8-5 (1)

NO ____138____ $ ____35.00____
DATE __April 1__ 20 ____
TO _Petty Cash_
FOR _To establish a Petty_
____Cash fund____

	DOLLARS	CENTS
BAL. BRO'T FOR'D	1406	92
AMT. DEPOSITED		
TOTAL	1406	92
AMT. THIS CHECK	35	00
BAL. CAR'D FOR'D	1371	92

No. __138__
1-830
960
__April 1__ 20____
Pay to the order of __Petty cash__ $ __35.00__
Thirty-five and ————— 00/100 Dollars

BOLTON NATIONAL BANK
of New York, NY

Hilda Marcello
(or Student's name)

⑈0860⸱⸱⸱0830⑈ 1843⸱⸱⸱671⑈'

8-5 (2)

No. __1__
SPACE TRAVEL SERVICES
Petty Cash Voucher

Date __April 2__ 20 _____

Pay to __Messenger__
For __Delivery Package__
____Delivery Expense____

Amount
$ 2.75

____XYZ____
Payment Received

____Student's Name____
Authorized

No. 2   SPACE TRAVEL SERVICES
Petty Cash Voucher

Date *April 9* 20 _____

Pay to *Post Office*
For *Postage*
     Office Expense

Amount
$ 8.00

     ABC
Payment Received

     Student's Name
Authorized

No. 3   SPACE TRAVEL SERVICES
Petty Cash Voucher

Date *April 16* 20 _____

Pay to *Employee name*
For *Gasoline*
     Auto Expense

Amount
$ 10.00

     JKL
Payment Received

     Student's Name
Authorized

No. 4   SPACE TRAVEL SERVICES
Petty Cash Voucher

Date *April 23* 20 _____

Pay to *Stationery Store*
For *Business cards*
     Misc. Expense

Amount
$ 7.50

     LMN
Payment Received

     Student's Name
Authorized

No. 5   SPACE TRAVEL SERVICES
                 Petty Cash Voucher

                              Date   April 30   20 _____

Pay to   Post Office
For   Postage   Amount
           Office Expense $ 4.00

_____   _____
         ABC   Student's Name
     Payment Received   Authorized

8-5 (3) sort:

Delivery Exp	Auto Exp	Office Exp	Misc Exp
$ 2.75	$10.00	$ 8.00	$7.50
		4.00	
		12.00	

Prove:

$ 2.75 $ 32.25 Vouchers
+10.00   2.75 Cash
+12.00 $35.00   Total of Petty Cash Fund
+ 7.50
$32.25 amount of replenishing check

8-5 (3)

NO _156_	$ _32.25_	SPACE TRAVEL SERVICES	No. _156_

	DOLLARS	CENTS
BAL. BRO'T FOR'D	1091	37
AMT. DEPOSITED	500	00
TOTAL	1591	37
AMT. THIS CHECK	32	25
BAL. CAR'D FOR'D	1559	12

NO _156_ $ _32.25_
DATE _April 30_   20 _____
TO _Petty Cash_
FOR _Auto Exp. 10.00—Del._
Exp. 2.75—Office Exp.
12.00—Misc. Exp. 7.50

SPACE TRAVEL SERVICES   No. _156_
                                                  1-830
                                                   860
                      April 30   20_____
Pay to the
order of   Cash $ _32.25_

Thirty-two and ——————————————— $\frac{25}{100}$ Dollars

BOLTON NATIONAL BANK
   of New York, NY   Hilda Marcello
                                           (or student's name)

⑈0860⋯0830⑈ 1243⋯671⑈

8-6

20__ Apr.	1	Petty cash							3 5 00											
		Cash										3 5 00
		To establish fund										
	30	Auto Expense							1 0 00				
		Delivery Expense							2 75				
		Miscellaneous Expense							7 50				
		Office Expense							1 2 00				
		Cash										3 2 25
		To replenish fund										

THINK IT OVER

1. Hankins assumes no legal responsibility by his qualified endorsement. The bank may attempt to recover from the drawer of the check who had insufficient funds in his/her checking account.

2. Responsibility should be separated between the drawer of checks from the regular checking account and the person in charge of the petty cash fund. If the fund requires frequent replenishment, it should be increased to a larger amount. The owner might also set a limit on the dollar amount of expenditures which can be paid from the petty cash fund.

Chapter 9

QUESTIONS

1. A service type of business sells the services to be performed—plumbing, electrical, TV repair, and the like. (A merchandising business sells goods—clothing, appliances, furniture, and such.)

2. A purchases journal is used to record the purchase of merchandise on account.

3. Creditors' accounts are arranged alphabetically in a subsidiary ledger.

4. Instead of listing each creditor's account in the general ledger, a control account—Accounts Payable—with a credit balance will maintain the equality of debits and credits.

5. The sum of all creditors' account balances should equal the balance of the control account—Accounts Payable—in the general ledger.

6. A three-column ruling in ledger accounts indicates the balance of each account with a minimum of adding and subtracting.

PROBLEMS

9–1 (1) and (3)

PURCHASES JOURNAL   *Page 5*

Date		From Whom Purchased Account Credited		Invoice No.	PR	Purchases Dr. Acct. Pay. Cr.
20__ Feb.	3	Dye & Akins		1705	✓	300 00
	10	Edward Kalpakian & Sons		G-116	✓	425 00
	17	Dye & Akins		1751	✓	385 00
	25	Edward Kalpakian & Sons		G-151	✓	500 00
	28	Total				1610 00
						(51) (21)

9–1 (2)

ACCOUNTS PAYABLE LEDGER

Dye & Akins
1011 Mountain Avenue, Denver, CO 80201

Date			PR	Dr.	Cr.	Cr. Bal
20__ Jan.	15		P1		450 00	450 00
Feb.	3		P5		300 00	750 00
	17		P5		385 00	1135 00

Edward Kalpakian & Sons
379 Valley View Drive, Denver, CO 80204

Date			PR	Dr.	Cr.	Cr. Bal
20__ Feb.	10		P5		425 00	425 00
	25		P5		500 00	925 00

9–1 (3)

Account No. 21
Accounts Payable

Date		Explanation	PR	Debit	Credit	Balance
Jan.	31		P1		450	450
Feb.	28		P5		1610	2060

Account No. 51
Purchases

Date		Explanation	PR	Debit	Credit	Balance
Feb.	28		P5	1610		1610

9–1 (4)

	Ruth Ann Davis	
	Schedule of Accounts Payable	
	February 28, 20__	

Dye & Akins		1 1 3 5 00
Edward Kalpakian & Sons		9 2 5 00
Total Accounts Payable		2 0 6 0 00

9–2 (1) and (3)

PURCHASES JOURNAL   Page 2

Date		From Whom Purchased Account Credited		Invoice No.	PR	Purchases Dr. Acct. Pay. Cr.
20__ Feb.	1	Paul Olins		#42	✓	1 7 5 00
	5	Wilson & Shea		513	✓	2 0 0 00
	8	Island Supply		72A	✓	2 6 5 00
	12	Wilson & Shea		543	✓	4 0 0 00
	15	Glen Mfg. Inc.		31	✓	6 2 0 00
	19	Paul Olins		78	✓	3 6 0 00
	22	Gregory Sims		318	✓	2 5 0 00
	26	Island Supply		29B	✓	3 0 0 00
	28	Total				2 5 7 0 00
						(51) (21)

9–2 (2)

ACCOUNTS PAYABLE LEDGER
Glen Mfg. Inc.

Date			PR	Debit	Credit	Balance
20__ Feb.	15		P2		620 00	620 00

Island Supply

Date			PR	Debit	Credit	Balance
20__ Feb.	8		P2		265 00	265 00
	26		P2		300 00	565 00

Paul Olins

Date			PR	Debit	Credit	Balance
20__ Feb.	1		P2		175 00	175 00
	19		P2		360 00	535 00

Gregory Sims

Date			PR	Debit	Credit	Balance
20__ Feb.	22		P2		250 00	250 00

Wilson & Shea

Date			PR	Debit	Credit	Balance
20__ Feb.	5		P2		200 00	200 00
	12		P2		400 00	600 00

9–2 (3)

Account No. 21
Accounts Payable

Date		Explanation	PR	Debit	Credit	Balance
Feb.	28		P2		2570	2570

Account No. 51
Purchases

Date		Explanation	PR	Debit	Credit	Balance
Feb.	28		P2	2570		2570

9–2 (4)

Maria Zagretti
Schedule of Accounts Payable
February 28, 20__

Glen Mfg., Inc.		620 00
Island Supply		565 00
Paul Olins		535 00
Gregory Sims		250 00
Wilson & Shea		600 00
Total Accounts Payable		2570 00

THINK IT OVER

Marino does not have to post to the purchases account for each purchase. Instead, he posts once from the total of the purchases journal.

Chapter 10

QUESTIONS

1. A special journal for cash disbursements reduces the amount of time and expense in posting credits to the cash account. Only one posting is made at the end of the fiscal period for a credit to Cash.

2. Postings from the cash disbursements journal are identified by the letters *CD* and page number.

3. How often an account title is used determines the use of a special column.

4. Special column totals will have account numbers as posting references to general ledger accounts; other account postings will be indicated by an account number or a check mark.

5. A check mark indicates "do not post" for a general Dr. column total.

6. A check mark for a subsidiary account indicates that the item has been posted.

7. The sum of all subsidiary accounts at the end of a fiscal period should equal the balance of the control account in the general ledger.

PROBLEMS

10-1 (1) and (2)

CASH DISBURSEMENTS JOURNAL   *Page 3*

Date	Account Credited	Ck. No.	PR	General Dr.	Acct. Pay. Dr.	S. Krasnoff Draw. Dr.	Cash Cr.
20__							
Mar. 1	Rent Expense	247		400 00			400 00
3	Utilities Expense	248		76 50			76 50
8	Paula Cory	249			50 00		50 00
10		250				500 00	500 00
17	Salary Expense	251		300 00			300 00
22	Hilda Piper	252			90 00		90 00
24		253				500 00	500 00
29	Equipment	254		1250 00			1250 00
31	Salary Expense	255		300 00			300 00
31	Totals			2326 50	140 00	1000 00	3466 50
				(✓)	( )	( )	( )

10-2 (1) (3) and (4)

PURCHASES JOURNAL   Page 2

Date		From Whom Purchased Account Credited	Invoice No.	PR	Purchases Dr. Acct. Pay. Cr.
20__ Apr.	4	Abel & Jenks	P-311	✓	600 00
	20	W. T. Gross	5-113	✓	1450 00
	30	Total			2050 00
					(51) (21)

10-2 (1) (3) and (4)

CASH DISBURSEMENTS JOURNAL   Page 3

Date		Acct. Dr.	Ck. No.	PR	General Dr.	Acct. Pay Dr.	Cash Cr.
20__ Apr.	1	Rent Expense	502	64	450 00		450 00
	8	Helen Scordas, Drawing	503	32	400 00		400 00
	14	Abel & Jenks	504	✓		800 00	800 00
	15	Salary Expense	505	65	325 00		325 00
	22	Supplies	506	14	75 00		75 00
	28	Helen Scordas, Drawing	507	32	500 00		500 00
	30	W. T. Gross	508	✓		725 00	7250 00
	30	Totals			1750 00	1525 00	3275 00
					(✓)	(21)	(11)

10-2 (2) and (3)

Account No. 11
Cash

Date		Explanation	PR	Debit	Credit	Balance
Apr.	1	Balance				4500
Apr.	30		CD3		3275	1225

Account No. 14
Supplies

Date		Explanation	PR	Debit	Credit	Balance
Apr.	1	Balance				50
Apr.	22		CD3	75		125

Account No. 21
Accounts Payable

Date		Explanation	PR	Debit	Credit	Balance
Apr.	1	Balance				800
Apr.	30		P2		2050	2850
Apr.	30		CD3	1525		1325

Account No. 32
Scordas, Drawing

Date		Explanation	PR	Debit	Credit	Balance
Apr.	8		CD3	400		400
Apr.	28		CD3	500		900

Account No. 51
Purchases

Date		Explanation	PR	Debit	Credit	Balance
Apr.	30		P2	2050		2050

Account No. 64
Rent Expenses

Date		Explanation	PR	Debit	Credit	Balance
Apr.	1		CD3	450		450

Account No. 65
Salaries Expenses

Date		Explanation	PR	Debit	Credit	Balance
Apr.	15		CD3	325		325

10-2 (4)

ACCOUNTS PAYABLE LEDGER

Abel & Jenks

1200 Mineral Boulevard, Scranton, PA 18501

Date			PR	Dr.	Cr.	Cr. Bal.
20__ Apr.	1	Balance	✓			80000
	4		P2		60000	140000
	14		CD3	80000		60000

W. T. Gross

805 Keystone Road, Wilkes Barre, PA 18700

Date			PR	Dr.	Cr.	Cr. Bal.
20__ Apr.	20		P2		145000	145000
	30		CD3	72500		72500

10-2 (5)

Helen Scordas

Schedule of Accounts Payable

April 30, 20__

Abel & Jenks		60000
W. T. Gross		72500
Total Accounts Payable		132500

Chapter 11

QUESTIONS

1. Sales of merchandise on account are recorded in a sales journal.

2. Customers' accounts may be arranged alphabetically or numerically in a subsidiary ledger.

3. Instead of listing each customer's account in the general ledger, a control account—Accounts Receivable—with a debit balance, will maintain the equality of debits and credits.

4. The total of all customers' accounts in the subsidiary ledger should equal the balance of the control account (Accounts Receivable) in the general ledger.

5. A small business might have fewer customers to whom merchandise is sold on account. It is easier to use their name as a reference because it does not require the business to set up a numbering system and a method for tracking those account numbers.

6. Sales invoice numbers are in consecutive order in the sales journal because they are numbered that way on the form used for such sales. Businesses use prenumbered documents as an internal control measure to prevent unauthorized use and to track any missing forms.

PROBLEMS

11-1 (1) and (3)

SALES JOURNAL   *Page 31*

Date		To Whom Sold - Account Debited	Invoice No.	PR	Accts. Rec. Dr. Sales Cr.
20__ Mar.	2	Mrs. Edward Ardyce	215	✓	175 00
	9	Mr. Herman Gold	216	✓	96 50
	16	Ms. Eliza Fisher	217	✓	107 30
	23	Mrs. Edward Ardyce	218	✓	62 45
	30	Ms. Eliza Fisher	219	✓	29 50
	31	Total			470 75
					(12) (42)

11-1 (2)

ACCOUNTS RECEIVABLE LEDGER

Mrs. Edward Ardyce
305 Riverview Terrace, Cincinnati, OH 45204

20__				Dr.	Cr.	Dr. Bal.
Mar.	2		S31	1 75 00		1 75 00
	23		S31	62 45		2 37 45

Ms. Eliza Fisher
851 Clarkfield Street, Cincinnati, OH 45201

20__				Dr.	Cr.	Dr. Bal.
Mar.	16		S31	1 07 30		1 07 30
	30		S31	29 50		1 36 80

Mr. Herman Gold
79 Willowbrook Drive, Cincinnati, OH 45202

20__				Dr.	Cr.	Dr. Bal.
Mar.	1	Balance	✓			2 58 60
	9		S31	96 50		3 55 10

11-1 (3)

GENERAL LEDGER

Accounts Receivable   No. 13

				Dr.	Cr.	Balance
20__ Mar.	1	Balance	✓			2 5 8 60
	9		S31	4 7 0 75		7 2 9 35

Sales   No. 41

				Dr.	Cr.	Balance
20__ Mar.	31		S31		4 7 0 75	4 7 0 75

11-1 (4)

Mears Department Store
Schedule of Accounts Receivable
March 31, 20__

Mrs. Edward Ardyce		2 3 7 45
Ms. Eliza Fisher		1 3 6 80
Mr. Herman Gold		3 5 5 10
Total Accounts Receivable		7 2 9 35

11-2 (1) and (3)

SALES JOURNAL

Page 8

Date		To Whom Sold–Account Debited	Invoice No.	PR	Accts. Rec. Dr. Sales Cr.
20__ Mar.	2	Mrs. Fay Wilamowski	328	✓	47 50
	6	Ms. Shirley Callahan	329	✓	36 20
	9	Mr. William Witt	330	✓	49 20
	13	Shirley Callahan	331	✓	107 20
	16	Mrs. Marjorie Intrator	332	✓	76 20
	20	Fay Wilamowski	333	✓	52 90
	23	William Witt	334	✓	59 20
	27	Marjorie Intrator	335	✓	67 75
	30	Shirley Callahan	336	✓	87 00
	30	Total			585 00
					(12)(42)

11-2 (2)

ACCOUNTS RECEIVABLE LEDGER
Ms. Shirley Callahan
186 Mineola Boulevard, Mineola, NY 11501

Date			PR	Dr.	Cr.	Dr. Bal
20__ Apr	1	Balance	✓			45 00
	6		S8	36 95		81 95
	13		S8	107 65		189 60
	30		S8	87 00		276 60

Mrs. Marjorie Intrator
91 Bryn Mawr, New Hyde Park, NY 11501

20__ Apr	16		S8	76 80		76 80
	27		S8	67 75		144 55

Mrs. Fay Wilamowski
451 Cornell Drive, Hicksville, NY 11803

20__ Apr	1	Balance	✓			65 30
	2		S8	47 50		112 80
	20		S8	52 90		165 70

Mr. William Witt
264 Emory Road, Mineola, NY 11501

20__ Apr	1	Balance	✓			95 00
	9		S8	49 25		144 25
	23		S8	59 20		203 45

11-2 (3)

Account No. 12
Accounts Receivable

Date		Explanation	PR	Debit	Credit	Balance
Apr.	*1*	*Balance*				*205.30*
Apr.	*30*		*S8*	*585.00*		*790.30*

Account No. 42
Sales

Date		Explanation	PR	Debit	Credit	Balance
Apr.	*30*		*S8*		*585.00*	*585.00*

11-2 (4)

Winslow's Emporium		
Schedule of Accounts Receivable		
April 30, 20__		

Ms. Shirley Callahan			276 60
Mrs. Marjorie Intrator			144 55
Mrs. Fay Wilamowski			165 70
Mr. William Witt			203 45
Total Accounts Receivable			790 30

THINK IT OVER

Marshall & Kahn will have better control of their records by using special journals. Time spent on posting from the journal to the ledger will be significantly reduced.

Chapter 12

QUESTIONS

1. All transactions that would result in debits to cash are entered in the cash receipts journal.

2. A special column would be used if the account for which cash is received is used frequently.

3. Special column total postings are indicated by general ledger account numbers; other account postings are indicated by check marks for subsidiary ledger accounts or numbers for general ledger accounts.

4. Check marks for subsidiary ledger accounts indicate that they have been posted.

5. Check marks for general Cr. column totals indicate that they should not be posted.

6. The sum of all customers' account balances in the subsidiary ledger should equal the balance of the control account—Accounts Receivable—in the general ledger.

PROBLEMS

12-1 (1) and (2)

CASH RECEIPTS JOURNAL

Page 6

Date		Account Credited	PR	General Cr.	Accts. Rec. Cr.	Sales Cr.	Cash Dr.
20__ Apr	23		✓	750 00	1435 00	5976 00	8161 00
	23	Raul Garcia, Capital		2000 00			2000 00
	24	Notes Payable		2500 00			2500 00
	25	J.R. Dallas			85 00		85 00
	26	Margo Chase			60 00		60 00
	27	Equipment		95 00			95 00
	28	Frances Lima			75 00		75 00
	29					1765 00	1765 00
	30	Totals		5345 00	1655 00	7741 00	14741 00
				(✓)	(12)	(42)	(11)

(Note: In a complete problem, items listed in the
General Cr. and Accts. Rec. Cr. columns
would be posted. Post references
would appear, therefore, in the PR column.)

12-1 (3)

Account No. 11
Cash

Date		Explanation	PR	Debit	Credit	Balance
Apr.	1	Balance				1935.00
Apr.	30		CR6	14741.00		16676.00

Account No. 12
Accounts Receivable

Date		Explanation	PR	Debit	Credit	Balance
Apr.	1	Balance				1729.50
Apr.	30		CR6		1655.00	74.50

Account No. 42
Sales

Date		Explanation	PR	Debit	Credit	Balance
Apr.	30		CR6		7741.00	7741.00

12-2 (1) and (2)

Sales Journal   Page 9

Date		To Whom Sold–Account Debited	Invoice No.	PR	Accts. Rec. Dr. Sales Cr.
20__ May	1	Willow's Beauty Shoppe	7156	✓	465 00
	1	Lee's Unisex	7157	✓	395 00
	12	Goddess of Love	7158	✓	268 50
	12	Jayne's Curls & Waves	7159	✓	175 00
	17	Willow's Beauty Shoppe	7160	✓	192 00
	29	Jayne's Curls & Waves	7161	✓	225 00
	29	Lee's Unisex	7162	✓	315 20
	31	Total			2035 70
					(12)(42)

12-2 (1) and (2)

CASH RECEIPTS JOURNAL
Page 6

Date		Account Credited	PR	General Cr.	Accts. Rec. Cr.	Sales Cr.	Cash Dr.
20__ May	7					252 50	252 50
	10	Goddess of Love	✓		200 00		200 00
	14					307 25	307 25
	15	Pat Norrell, Capital	31	3000 00			3000 00
	19	Lee's Unisex	✓		395 00		395 00
	21					296 80	296 80
	25	Willow's Beauty Shoppe	✓		265 00		265 00
	28					319 90	319 90
	31					191 40	191 40
	31	Totals		3000 00	860 00	1367 85	5227 85
				(✓)	(12)	(42)	(11)

12-2 (2)

Account No. 11
Cash

Date		Explanation	PR	Debit	Credit	Balance
May	1	Balance				1078.50
May	31		CR6	5227.85		6306.35

Account No. 12
Accounts Receivable

Date		Explanation	PR	Debit	Credit	Balance
May	1	Balance				200.00
May	31		S9	2035.70		2235.70
May	31		CR6		860.00	1375.70

Account No. 31
Capital

Date		Explanation	PR	Debit	Credit	Balance
May	1	Balance				25000.00
May	15		CR6		3000.00	28000.00

Account No. 42
Sales

Date		Explanation	PR	Debit	Credit	Balance
May	31		S9		2035.70	2035.70
May	31		CR6		1367.85	3403.55

12-2 (3)

ACCOUNTS RECEIVABLE LEDGER

Goddess of Love
110 Chemung Avenue, Binghamton, NY 13901

Date			PR	Dr.	Cr.	Dr. Bal
20__ May	1	Balance	✓			200 00
	10		CR6		200 00	–0–
	12		S9	268 50		268 50

Jayne's Curls & Waves
39 Tompkins Avenue, Cortland, NY 13045

Date			PR	Dr.	Cr.	Dr. Bal
20__ May	12		S9	175 00		175 00
	29		S9	225 00		400 00

Lee's Unisex
451 College Heights Road, Ithaca, NY 14850

Date			PR	Dr.	Cr.	Dr. Bal
20__						
May	1		S9	395 00		395 00
	19		CR6		395 00	–0–
	29		S9	315 20		315 20

Willow's Beauty Shoppe
58 Twain Boulevard, Elmira, NY 14901

Date			PR	Dr.	Cr.	Dr. Bal
20__						
May	1		S9	465 00		465 00
	17		S9	192 00		657 00
	25		CR6		265 00	392 00

12-2 (4)

Pat Norrell
Schedule of Accounts Receivable
May 31, 20__

Goddess of Love		268 50
Jayne's Curls & Waves		400 00
Lee's Unisex		315 20
Willow's Beauty Shoppe		392 00
Total Accounts Receivable		1375 70

Chapter 13

QUESTIONS

1. Sales are first recorded at full price because the discounts are optional and the seller does not know if the buyer will take the discount until payment is received.

2. Companies offer sales discounts so that their customers will pay sooner, thus improving cash flow.

3. All entries not entered in special journals are recorded in a general journal. Some examples are: adjusting entries, closing entries, and returns of merchandise on account.

4. Jones' Records:

Sales Returns and Allowances	$30
Accounts Receivable—Claire Smith	$30
Smith's Records:	
Accounts Payable—Henry Jones	$30
Purchase Returns and Allowances	$30

5. A credit memorandum is the source document for Jones' entry and a debit memorandum for Smith's entry.

6. A statement of account lists a customer's charges and payments and returns, with a balance due.

PROBLEMS

13-1 (1)

GENERAL JOURNAL   *Page 7*

Date		Description	PR	Debit	Credit
May	2	Sales Returns & Allowances		35 00	
		Accounts Receivable – Jane Mc Donald			35 00
	14	Accounts Payable – Baldwin Piano Co.		100 00	
		Purchase Returns & Allowances			100 00
	22	Sales Returns & Allowances		80 00	
		Accounts Receivable – Molly Shapiro			80 00

CASH RECEIPTS JOURNAL — Page 12

Date	Acct. Cr.	PR	General Cr.	Acct. Rec. Cr.	Sales Discount Dr.	Cash Dr.
May 15	M. Hill			150 00	3 00	147 00

CASH DISBURSEMENTS JOURNAL — Page 11

Date	Acct. Dr.	Ck. No.	PR	General Dr.	Accts. Pay. Dr.	Purch. Discount Cr.	Cash Cr.
May 23	Baldwin Piano Co.	1001			3200 00	96 00	3104 00

SALES JOURNAL — Page 14

Date	Account Debited	PR	Acct. Rec. Dr. Sales Cr.
May 5	M. Hill		150 00

13-2

GENERAL JOURNAL
Page 7

Date		Description	PR	Debit	Credit
20__ May	3	Accounts Payable – Home Decorator's Corp.		16000	
		Purchase Returns & Allowances			16000
May	17	Sales Returns & Allowances		7700	
		Accts. Receivable – R. Moore			7700

CASH RECEIPTS JOURNAL
Page 12

Date		Acct. Cr.	PR	General Cr.	Accts. Rec. Cr.	Sales Cr.	Cash Dr.
20__ May	24	Purchase Ret. & Allow.		5000			5000
	28	Accts. Pay. – Wilton Fabric		14000			14000

CASH DISBURSEMENTS JOURNAL
Page 11

Date		Acct. Dr.	Ck. No.	PR	General Dr.	Accts. Pay. Dr.	Purchases Dr.	Cash Cr.
20__ May	10	Sales Ret. & Allow.	326		3800			3800

13-3

STATEMENT OF ACCOUNT

Hudson's Department Store
100 Gateway Plaza
St. Louis, MO 63101

SOLD TO   May 20, 20___

Ms. Pearl Nathanson
972 Riverside Dr.
St. Louis, MO 63104

		CHARGES		
May	1		60 00	
	5		75 00	
	18		45 00	
				180 00
		PAYMENTS/RETURNS		
	12		35 00	
	15		20 00	
				55 00
	18	Balance Due		125 00

13-4 (1) and (2)

PURCHASES JOURNAL   Page 10

Date		Account Credited	Invoice No.	PR	Purchases Dr. Acct. Pay. Cr.			
20__								
May	17	Schmidt & Brendle				3	7	5	00
	17	Winston Jewelers			1	2	0	0	00
	31	Totals			1	5	7	5	00
					( )			( )

13-4 (1) and (2)

SALES JOURNAL   Page 14

Date		Account Debited	Invoice No.	PR	Accts. Rec. Dr. Sales Cr.			
20__								
May	4	Antonio Lorenzo	B192		3	0	0	00
	4	Edward Grabczak	B193		2	5	0	00
	11	Marc Green	B194		2	7	5	00
	31	Totals			8	2	5	00
					( )			( )

13-4 (1) and (2)

CASH RECEIPTS JOURNAL — Page 19

Date			PR	General Cr.	Accts. Rec Cr.	Sales Cr.	Cash Dr.
20__ May	3	Marc Green			150 00		150 00
	3	Gian Polidoro			95 00		95 00
	22	Antonio Lorenzo			50 00		50 00
	23	Edward Grabczak			125 00		125 00
	31		✓			2740 00	2740 00
	31	Totals		—	420 00	2740 00	3160 00
				(✓)	( )	( )	( )

13-4 (1) and (2)

CASH DISBURSEMENTS JOURNAL — Page 17

Date			Ck. No.	PR	General Dr.	Accts. Pay. Dr.	Purchases Dr.	Cash Cr.
20__ May	1	Winslow Jewelers	392			465 00		465 00
	1	Rent Expense	393		450 00			450 00
	13	Daniel Shaw, Drawing	394		500 00			500 00
	14	Salary Expense	395		300 00			300 00
	28	Schmidt & Brendle	396			375 00		375 00
	29	Sales Returns & Allowances	397		40 00			40 00
	31	Totals			1290 00	840 00	—	2130 00
					(✓)	( )	—	( )

13-4 (1) and (2)

GENERAL JOURNAL Page 12

Date		Description	PR	Debit	Credit
May	8	Supplies		3500	
		Equipment			3500
		Error Correction			
May	24	Sales Returns & Allowances		7500	
		Accounts Receivable – Marc Green			7500
May	31	Equipment		20000	
		Accounts Payable – Allen Co.			20000

Chapter 14

QUESTIONS

1. The heading includes the company name, the report title, and the date.

2. The three sections of the income statement are revenues, cost of goods sold, and operating expenses.

3. Shipping costs are included in the total cost of purchasing merchandise.

4. Using the closing entries, beginning inventory is credited to remove it, and ending inventory is debited to record it.

PROBLEMS

14-1 (a)

Net Sales = Sales − Sales Discounts − Sales Returns and Allowances
(1,000 − 30 − 20) = 950

14-1 (b)

Net Purchases = Purchases − Purchase discounts − Purchase Returns and Allowances
$$(200 - 40 - 25) = 135$$

14-1 (c)

Cost of Goods Purchased = Net Purchases + Freight-In
$$(135 + 15) = 150$$

14-1 (d)

Goods Available for Sale = Beginning Inventory + Cost of Goods Purchased
$$(400 + 150) = 550$$

14-2

Jan's Appliance Warehouse
Income Statement
For the month ended July 31, 2010

Revenues:

Sales	$1,000		
Less: Sales Discounts	30		
Sales Returns and Allowances	20		
Net Sales			950

Cost of Goods Sold:

Merchandise Inventory, July 1		400	
Purchases	200		
Less: Purchase Discounts	40		
Purchase Returns and Allowances	25		
Net Purchases	135		
Add: Freight-In	15		
Cost of Goods Purchased		150	
Goods Available for Sale		550	
Less: Merchandise Inventory, July 31		300	
Cost of Goods Sold			250
Gross Profit			700

Operating Expenses:

Advertising Expense	20	
Rent Expense	100	
Salary Expense	150	
Supplies Expense	10	
Total Operating Expenses		280
Net Income		$420

14-3

Date	Description	PR	Debit	Credit
	Merchandise Inventory		3000 00	
	Sales		10000 00	
	Purchase Discounts		40 00	
	Purchase Returns & Allowances		25 00	
	Income Summary			13650 00
	Income Summary		9450 00	
	Sales Discounts			300 0
	Sales Returns & Allowances			200 0
	Purchases			2000 0
	Freight-In			150 0
	Advertising Expense			200 0
	Rent Expense			1000 0
	Salary Expense			1500 0
	Supplies Expense			100 0
	Merchandise Inventory			4000 0
	Income Summary		4200 0	
	Jan's Capital			4200 0
	Jan's Capital		500 0	
	Jan's Drawings			500 0

Chapter 15

QUESTIONS

1. Two popular accounting software packages are QuickBooks and Peachtree.

2. Some advantages of using a computerized system are:
   a. Convenience
   b. Ease of use
   c. Time savings
   d. Reasonable cost
   e. Error reduction
   f. Improved management information

3. Posting is accomplished by clicking on the Post button.

4. Reports can help the manager/owner by providing timely, accurate, and detailed feedback on the business's operations.

PART TWO EXAMINATION

PART I

1.	T	11.	F
2.	T	12.	T
3.	T	13.	F
4.	F	14.	F
5.	F	15.	T
6.	T	16.	F
7.	T	17.	F
8.	F	18.	T
9.	F	19.	T
10.	T	20.	T

PART II

1.	M	7.	L
2.	J	8.	A
3.	N	9.	I
4.	C	10.	O
5.	D	11.	H
6.	F		

PART III

(1)

GENERAL JOURNAL

Page 7

Date		Description	PR	Debit	Credit
20__					
June	8	Glaser, Drawing		50 00	
		Purchases			50 00
	12	Sales Returns & Allowances		15 00	
		Accounts Receivable – George Tyler	/		15 00

PART III

(1) and (2)

PURCHASES JOURNAL

Page 3

Date		Account Credited	PR	Purchases Dr. Accts. Pay. Cr.
20__				
June	3	J. L. Rossini Company		5 0 0 00
	29	Fred Pulaski Wholesalers, Inc.		3 0 0 00
	30	Total		8 0 0 00
				( ) ( )

PART III
(1) and (2)

SALES JOURNAL   Page 3

Date		Account Debited	Invoice No.	PR	Accts. Rec. Dr. Sales Cr.
20__ June	5	Dr. George Tyler	452		1 6 5 00
	26	Sonia Parisian	453		1 2 5 00
	30	Total			2 9 0 00
					( ) ( )

PART III
(1) and (2)

CASH RECEIPTS JOURNAL   Page 4

Date		Account Credited	PR	General Cr.	Accts. Rec. Cr.	Sales Cr.	Cash Dr.
20__ June	15		✓			2950 00	2950 00
	22	Dr. George Tyler			150 00		150 00
	30		✓			3750 00	3750 00
	30	Totals			150 00	6700 00	6850 00
				(✓)	( )	( )	( )

PART III

(1) and (2)

Page 3

CASH DISBURSEMENTS JOURNAL

Date		Account Debited	Ck. No.	PR	General Dr.	Accts. Pay. Dr.	Purchases Dr.	Salary Exp. Dr.	Cash Cr.
20__ June	1	Rent Expense	147		375 00				375 00
	10	J. L. Rossini Company	148			500 00			500 00
	19	Telephone Expense	149		46 00				46 00
	30	Totals			421 00	500 00			921 00
					(✓)	( )			( )

PART IV

(1)

Annie's Flower Emporium
Income Statement
For the month ended August 31, 2010

Revenues:

Sales		$13,000	
Less: Sales Discounts	230		
Sales Returns and Allowances	125	455	
Net Sales			12,645

Cost of Goods Sold:

Merchandise Inventory, August 1		1,600	
Purchases	8,000		
Less: Purchase Discounts	130		
Purchase Returns and Allowances	550		
Net Purchases		7,320	
Add: Freight-In		300	
Cost of Goods Purchased		7,620	
Goods Available for Sale		9,220	
Less: Merchandise Inventory, August 31		1,500	
Cost of Goods Sold			7,720
Gross Profit			4,925

Operating Expenses:

Advertising Expense	400	
Insurance Expense	200	
Miscellaneous Expense	180	
Rent Expense	650	
Salaries Expense	900	
Supplies Expense	125	
Total Operating Expenses		2,455
Net Income		$2,470

PART IV

(2)

1.

		Closing Entries						
		Merchandise Inventory			1 50 0 00			
		Sales			13 00 0 00			
		Purchase Discounts			1 30 00			
		Purchase Returns & Allowances			5 50 00			
		Income Summary					15 18 0 00	

2.

		Closing Entries						
		Income Summary			12 71 0 00			
		Sales Discounts					2 30 00	
		Sales Returns & Allowances					1 25 00	
		Purchases					8 00 0 00	
		Freight-In					3 00 00	
		Advertising Expense					4 00 00	
		Insurance Expense					2 00 00	
		Miscellaneous Expense					1 80 00	
		Rent Expense					6 50 00	
		Salaries Expense					9 00 00	
		Supplies Expense					1 25 00	
		Merchandise Inventory					1 60 0 00	

3.

		Closing Entries						
		Income Summary			2 47 0 00			
		Annie's Capital					2 47 0 00	

4.

		Closing Entries						
		Annie's Capital			2 00 00			
		Annie's Drawings					2 00 00	

INDEX